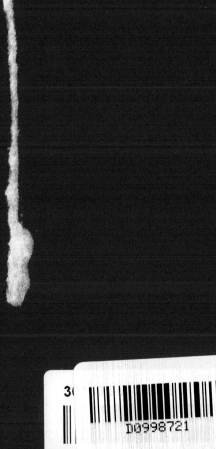

2014

2014

How to Survive the Next World Crisis

Nicholas Boyle

continuum

Published by the Continuum International Publishing Group

The Tower Building
11 York Road
London
SE1 7NX

80 Maiden Lane
Suite 704
New York
NY 10038

www.continuumbooks.com

First published 2010

British Library Cataloguing-in-Publication Data
A catalogue record for this book is available from the British Library.

ISBN 978-1441-18509-9

Designed and typeset by Pindar NZ, Auckland, New Zealand
Printed and bound by MPG Books Group

Contents

For Jim and Nigel

Acknowledgements

This book owes its existence to the urging, support, and wise advice of my wife, Rosemary: my gratitude to her goes beyond anything that can be said here. My thanks are also due to the many readers and audiences who by comments and questions have helped me to formulate my thoughts better, and especially to Jim Devlin and Nigel Morris, who have much improved the view from my ivory tower onto the battlefield of business.

Earlier or partial versions of chapters 1, 4, and 6 have appeared in *The Tablet*, of chapter 2 in *New Blackfriars*, of chapters 4 and 8 in *Journal of Law, Philosophy and Culture* (Vol. III No. 1 (2009) pp. 261–72) and of chapter 9 in *Ethical Perspectives*. I am grateful to the editors of these journals for permitting me to reproduce this material here. I owe a special word of thanks to Brendan Walsh for his kind, shrewd, and generous suggestions about both the text and its publication.

N.B.

Introduction

There can now be no doubt that in 2007 a series of events began of historical, indeed world-historical, importance. Whatever hopes there may be for a swift emergence of the Western nations from recession, it is obviously vain, after the destruction of 40 per cent of the world's wealth, to expect things to carry on much as before. The enormous quantities of debt incurred by American, British and European governments to stabilize their banks and stimulate their economies will burden domestic policy-making and international relations for many years to come. In the course of those years, either further enormous expenditure will be needed to avert climatic disaster or the disaster itself will become inevitable. As India and China, after two centuries of exclusion, resume their rightful place in the world system, the inequalities in the system – already apparent in the excessive deficits and surpluses that led to the recession and in the differential rates of growth leading out of it – will have to be reduced. The next world crisis will be not economic but political. A period of intense international negotiation lies ahead, of which the G20 meeting in April 2009 and the largely (but not completely) futile Copenhagen conference on climate change in December of that year are only the beginning. How those negotiations are concluded will determine the character of the world in which the next two or three generations of the human race will have to live.

Among the most important topics of negotiation will be the nature of the international order itself. In the twentieth century there was a presumption that the world was, or ought to be, made up of independent, autonomous nation-states. To a much greater extent than is generally realised, that presumption derived from the growing, and ultimately overwhelming, economic, military and political dominance of the USA, and the ideology on which the USA relied in order to explain to itself its own nationhood. The American ideology – perhaps it should really be called the American religion – prescribed that nation-states were voluntary associations of individuals endowed with unalienable rights. That is not a realistic basis either for understanding the global interdependence that grew up in the late twentieth century or for negotiating the settlement that in the twenty-first century will have to make up for the follies of the past and ensure us against an even more threatening future. In this book I attempt to show how we need to rethink the recent phase of globalization that brought us to our present pass; how in particular we all, Americans included, need to achieve some intellectual distance from the Americanist presuppositions underlying twentieth-century ideas about international relations; and how there are conceivable mechanisms, not utopian and not even far-fetched, that, for all the thunderclouds building around us, could make the world more equitable, peaceful and prosperous than it is at the moment.

The book is short, but I have still found it necessary to divide it into two parts. In the first I concentrate on the crisis that has already begun – its origins, and the nation-based concepts that prevent us from understanding it correctly – and on the moment of decision that lies ahead of us, when the deeper issues that have begun to make themselves felt can no longer be postponed and the character of the twenty-first century will be determined, for better or for worse. In the second part I attempt to deal with the broader and more theoretical questions that recent events have raised. Lord Turner has said that economic policy makers have to contemplate the 'fairly complete train wreck' of the 'intellectual system' in which they used to operate. Now is the time to try for a serious revision of the basis of our economic, political and ethical thinking, and to address – more productively, I hope, than hitherto – the question of national identity.

I admit that my title, and the starting point of my argument, is something of a joke. But the joke has a point. Historians have for some time now worked with the concept of overlapping 'long' centuries: a long seventeenth century ending around 1715, a long eighteenth century from 1688 to 1815 or even 1832, a long nineteenth century from 1789 to 1914. The long twenty-first century will no doubt prove to have begun in 1989, but the long twentieth century has still to end. It will be interesting to see when, and how, it does. We have probably not got long to wait.

Part I

Towards the Great Event

Chapter 1

The Great Event: A Numerological Speculation

With commentators everywhere scanning the future in the hope of discerning how the current financial and economic storm will develop, why should numerology be any less reliable than crystal-ball gazing? Ronald Knox built his masterpiece *Let Dons Delight* on a wonderful numerological fancy: a series of conversations held exactly half a century apart, in the years 38 and 88 of every century since the sixteenth, repeatedly catch English society in the moment of some decisive event or transition – whether the Spanish Armada or the Glorious English Revolution or the eve of its French counterpart. Knox ended his series, as he had to, in 1938 – heading his last chapter 'Chaos' – but a 1988 chapter would have fitted perfectly into his pattern: the Marxist dons would have been as comically unaware of the impending collapse of the Cold War order as their *ancien régime* equivalents in 1788.

But another, more sombre, numerological speculation is now becoming more pressing. It is striking how regularly, over the last 500 years, the character of a new century has been laid down by some event, both decisive and symbolic, occurring in the middle of the second decade: the Ninety-Five Theses, which began the Reformation in 1517; the outbreak of the Thirty Years' War in 1618, which began a century of religious and civil strife; the death of Louis XIV and the establishment of the Hanoverian succession in England in 1715, which, together with the treaties ending the war of Spanish succession, set the scene for an eighteenth century of European Enlightenment and British imperial expansion; the final defeat of Napoleon, and the Congress of Vienna, in 1815, which ushered in an age of peace and industrialization in Europe; the slide into 75 years of hot and cold world war in 1914.

Fancies need no justification. If one is thought to be necessary, though, it might be something like this: by 15 or 20 years into each new century, those born in the last decades of the old – say, in the '80s – are mature and influential enough to dispense with the heritage of the epoch that they never felt was their own. They are the parents, making the world that will be inhabited by their children – the generation that will live all its life in the new century – and whatever they do, hindsight will have to regard it as typical of the new age. To put it another way: if the new century is to have a character at all, it will have to be established by the time it is 20 years old.

So what will be the great event that between 2010 and 2020, probably around 2015, will both symbolize and determine the character of the twenty-first century? Will it be a disaster of the magnitude of 1618 or 1914, or the relatively benign conjuncture represented by 1715 and 1815? Whichever it is, it is likely that the present turmoil in the world economies is leading us up to that Great Event, which will either resolve the crisis of the next seven years or so or mark its catastrophic conclusion.

It is not difficult to guess the principal factors that will be involved in the making of the Great Event and that will characterize the century it will later be seen to have inaugurated. The competition for oil and other natural resources, including water; the environmental impact of industrial development, especially climate change; and the changing economic and geopolitical balance between the USA and China (with Russia playing an important but secondary role because of its energy resources and its still enormous but imperfectly controlled nuclear armoury) are the real lines of stress in the current global system. It would, I believe, be a mistake to include alongside them a supposed clash of 'Western' and 'Islamic' civilizations: that is certainly capable of providing the stage décor for a showdown (and Pakistan's nuclear thunderflashes are terribly real), but it is not a profound source of tension in the world, of the kind that moves economies and armies. The apparent significance of the Western–Islamic divide is a consequence of the dependence (in the drug-addicted sense) of the USA on Middle Eastern oil and of the disproportionate leverage on American foreign policy exercised by states in that region, from Saudi Arabia to Israel. If in the course of the twenty-first century that oil runs out, or alternative sources of either oil or energy in general become available, the late twentieth-century concern with the culture and politics of these small and otherwise unproductive countries will seem as obsolete as sixteenth- or seventeenth-century concerns for the control of the Spice Islands.

The profound shift that began in the late twentieth century and that the twenty-first will see completed – one way or another – is the integration into the global market for the world's resources, and for its man-made products, of one sixth of the human race (counting only China) or one third (if we include India) who previously survived in the isolation of subsistence economies. Such a shift, involving huge changes in the proportional distribution of wealth and influence, taking place at a time of increasing awareness that our planet is limited in its ability to sustain our current pattern of production and consumption, necessarily has political implications. That is to say, it has implications for the internal structure and external relations of the states into which the human race is organized, not by the power of economic interest but by the non-economic power of coercion – ultimately by force of arms. Changes in the distribution of economic activity across the world will change the balance of political and military power. By the middle of the next decade, it should be clear whether the necessary adjustments to the system of (formal or informal) international agreements by which the resort to military force is controlled can be made successfully, so that a new equilibrium is introduced. Alternatively, by about 2015 the existing centres of economic power will have shown that rather than cede or restructure influence they will, Samson-like, pull down the house upon us all. In numerological terms, we should then know whether the twenty-first century has begun with a new 1815 or a new 1914.

Maybe the period from the collapse of communism in 1989 to the Great Event around 2015 will come in retrospect to resemble the period from 1789 to 1815. During that turbulent transition new states came and went, a 900-year-old empire disappeared and the papacy was nearly extinguished. But once the shock of the French Revolution had been absorbed, a new system of British industrial and imperial hegemony was established – a first phase of a truly global capitalism – which brought relatively peaceful economic development to large areas of the world.

A more ominous parallel, however, would be with the end of that period of British hegemony. The unification of Germany in 1871 gave political shape to a growing economic counterweight to British power, which soon became a military counterweight as well. The inability of European and American statesmen to create a global political structure to contain and control the changing balance of global economic power was then horribly punished in 1914 and in the Seventy-Five Years' War that followed, in which the nineteenth-century empires were gradually dismembered at an enormous human cost.

Contemporary China bears an uncomfortable resemblance to late nineteenth-century Germany, and the international constellation in which this new star appears is also uncomfortably *déjà vu.* Imperial Germany was a late entrant into the club of industrializing nations, but inward investment from the older powers, notably Britain, had brought into being a more modern economy than theirs, the size and dynamism of which was soon a cause of their trepidation. On the whole, of course, economic competition is good for everybody, in the end. The trouble is caused in the medium term by the social and political friction it engenders. Whereas in Britain and America and, on the whole, in France, well-established representative institutions maintained a community of interest, and an overlap of personnel, between the classes who were making the money and the classes who furnished the political – and especially the military – leaders, Germany was a country with no modern democratic traditions, which had only partially emerged from an autocratic past, and whose political and military leadership was drawn from a single closed caste, the landed nobility, whose attitudes, traditions and interests were largely at odds with those of the newly wealthy bourgeoisie. This internally divided society was held together by an artificial ideology of German nationhood, in the interests of which the bourgeoisie were expected to subordinate their desire for political autonomy to their military rulers. These in turn were under increasing pressure to demonstrate their value to the nation (that is, to secure their own positions) by belligerent gestures and plans, which one day turned into disastrous reality. The arms race with Britain, seemingly still the dominant world power but economically already overtaken by the younger generation; the pointless but very rapid expansion of the German navy; and the symbolic acquisition of a number of colonies were international provocations prompted by the internal imperative – for the ruling class – to maintain the ideology of the nation and so keep the middle classes under control.

In the absence of an international framework to soothe the tensions, eliminate the unnecessary provocations and promote coordinated action to manage the underlying instabilities, economic competition developed into military confrontation, and for that transition all parties must bear the blame. The later obsession of the Allies with fixing war guilt on Germany was a deliberate repression of their own guilty knowledge that they had failed to submit their interests to the disagreeable discipline of supranational political bodies.

China now similarly looks like a newcomer to the global club who, fired up by investment from the older members, is set to outperform them all. It too has only recently emerged from autocratic and arbitrary rule and has no local tradition of representative government. Its rapidly expanding middle class is the source both of its new wealth and significance in the world and of grave anxiety to its political and military rulers, who maintain into a capitalist era the tradition of bureaucratic authoritarianism, under the name of communism, just as Germany's rulers maintained it under the name of monarchy. Like nineteenth-century Germany, too, China is an old culture which has suffered recent humiliation, and there is plenty of opportunity to rouse the nationalism, and even racism, deeply rooted in Han society, should the political and military authorities choose to play that card. They are almost as isolated from the moneymakers by the party structure as Germany's leaders were by hereditary nobility, and they too may feel they need the support of patriotic and belligerent gestures. Emboldened by their new economic power they may choose to square up to a USA they think is losing its grip, as Germany did to Britain. Nor should we set too much store by speculation on an end to single-party rule in China. Even if there were to be a Chinese revolution it would not necessarily improve the prospects for world peace. The current regime is probably more realistic, and certainly better informed, about the outside world than the majority of the Chinese electorate is ever likely to be. Bismarck after 1871 was a better guarantor of peace in Europe than the democratic constitution of the Weimar Republic. Moreover, America – feeling and fearing the loss of its preeminence, the rise in the cost of its energy and raw materials and the domestic disruption caused by international competition – may, as Britain did around 1900, accept the inevitability of confrontation and engage in a war of words which will eventually develop into war of a different kind. Taiwan is a permanent potential *casus belli* for either side, should they wish to bring matters to a decision.

Everything in the end may depend on whether America can react more imaginatively to a decline in relative economic power – to sharing with others both the world's resources and its own standard of living – than Britain was able to do in the years before 1914. It has the leeway to do so: its global military predominance is far greater than Britain's ever was. The turning point to disaster came relatively early in the history of Imperial Germany: in 1879, when America and Europe responded to the long depression, which had begun in 1873 with bank failures and stock crashes, by retreating into protectionism. We have perhaps learned the lesson that restraints on trade, quite apart from their economic consequences, reduce the potential area of international relations, ultimately to that of trials of military strength. The protectionist follies of the 1930s, which turned a crash into a depression and a depression into a world war, are still just about within living memory. We can perhaps now see that, in the trying times that are just beginning, the World Trade Organization (WTO) is more important than the United Nations to world peace. The danger signs over the next few years will be any retreat by the American administration from the WTO or the North American Free Trade Agreement (NAFTA) (especially if it claims to be speaking for the generation born in the 1980s), any marked upgrading of China's military capacity and any intensification of the ideological rhetoric (whether it is China telling the world about sovereignty, or America telling China about democracy) – and, of course, any rattling of sabres, or missiles, in the neighbourhood of Taiwan, Xinjiang, Pakistan or, just conceivably, Tibet.

But the choice between 1815 and 1914 remains open. It may be that the two greatest economic powers in the second decade of the twenty-first century, between which the financial links are now so strong, will see that an international structure is needed to control nuclear-armed mavericks, old and new, and to impose order on the demographic upheavals consequent on climate change. A crisis, even a violent crisis, resolved in that way would not, in the perspective of a century, be a disaster. It may, though, also be that pursuing the illusion of self-sufficiency in difficult times will bring on us even greater retribution than did the twentieth century, and that the Great Event, which is now fast approaching, will eclipse all its predecessors and leave few of us behind to worry about numerological patterns. Either the world changes for good, or it changes for good.

Chapter 2

What Went Wrong with Globalization

Our current woes are no doubt in some sense a consequence of the last 20 years of globalization. But
globalization is nothing new. There has been world trade
at least since the establishment of the Parthian Empire
in the second century BC made secure the silk routes
between China and Rome. Even in AD 1000, according
to a recent and surely definitive study by Ronald Findlay
and Kevin H. O'Rourke,[*] the entire Eurasian continent
and North Africa, which fell into seven distinct political
and cultural regions from Japan to Morocco and from
Iceland to Indonesia, was interconnected through the
Islamic region, which maintained economic links with

---

[*] Ronald Findlay and Kevin H. O'Rourke, *Power and Plenty. Trade, War,
and the World Economy in the Second Millennium* (Princeton: Princeton
University Press, 2007).

all the others. But in the Italian 'commercial revolution' of the thirteenth century the essential features of a new system started to become apparent. Thanks partly to their contacts with the Islamic world, which brought them such crucial tools as decimal numbering, the bank agent and the cheque (the word itself is probably Arabic in origin), the Italian city-states were able to found an international financial system that supported and facilitated trade across all the regions. Its innovations, such as joint stock companies, regular postal services, marine insurance and new bookkeeping principles that made it possible to distinguish income from capital, proved robust and flexible enough to survive the economic downturn of the late Middle Ages and to support the early modern European explorations and imperial expansions that followed. The year 1776 saw not only the American colossus begin to stir but also Lloyd's of London formulate the master policy which was literally to underwrite the second British commercial empire and which, as Peter Spufford has shown,[*] is a direct descendant, through the insurance markets of Bruges and Barcelona, of the Italian policies of the fourteenth century. The thirteenth-century 'rents revolution', the replacement of feudal dues by payments in coin, began the monetarization of European social relations,

---

[*] Peter Spufford, *Power and Profit: The Merchant in Medieval Europe* (London: Thames and Hudson, 2003).

which made possible the deployment by the empire-builders of domestic capital in foreign trade. Around 1800, the world economy began to change fundamentally when growth in the volume and complexity of trading relations accelerated as a result of Europe's Industrial Revolution. The last 800 years – not a long time in the life of the human species – have seen the continuous growth, fitful at first but never definitively interrupted, of a system of commerce, finance and communications which has brought more and more human beings into economic, technical and cultural relations with one another. No later than the middle of the nineteenth century, and arguably considerably earlier, that system gave certain privileged centres – now very much more numerous – a range of knowledge and influence that literally encompassed the planet and put them potentially in a relationship with every member of the species. By about 1870, this process of increasing international economic interaction passed into a qualitatively new phase in which it deserves the name of 'globalization'. Already in 1848 the *Communist Manifesto* had predicted the advent of a global market, a *Weltmarkt*; but in the last third of the nineteenth century, technological change in transport and communications and the completion of the last great journeys of European discovery realized that prediction by establishing a system of global, that is, planetary, and not just international, trade. At the same time, the imperialist race for territory accelerated as it became a matter of practical concern that the world is a limited whole and the resources within it are limited. The symbolic moment of definition was the Washington conference of 1884, which made the Greenwich meridian into the baseline for a conceptual grid embracing the world and accepted by the world. As often happens, though, the imagination of the poets had anticipated the scientists and statesmen. The sense of a new and global unity runs through Jules Verne's *Around the World in Eighty Days*, published in 1872–3. The dénouement of Verne's tale depends on the paradoxes of the soon-to-be-fixed system of imaginary cartographic lines – a system which was also soon to determine physical and human reality in the preposterously arbitrary frontiers drawn by worldwide empires, particularly in Africa.

For all the venomous associations of the word 'capitalism' – a term coined by communists to create the impression that they were fighting against another ideology like their own, rather than against the facts of life – there can be no doubt that the fundamental character of the global economic order of the nineteenth and twentieth centuries was benign. If any historical thesis can be disproved, it is the claim that the extension and liberalization of world trade has been productive of extreme poverty. In the nearly two centuries since the end of the Napoleonic Wars – in the period, that is, in which the modern international economic system has been developing and taking on its global dimension – it has been possible for the number of human beings on the planet to multiply nearly sixfold. That in itself must be a good, even on fairly utilitarian criteria, and it is certainly a very great good if one believes that life itself is not just good but sacred. During that same period, however, the proportion of the world population in extreme poverty, as defined by the World Bank, has been steadily declining, from about 85 per cent in 1820 to 75 per cent in 1870 to 24 per cent in 1992. There are obviously serious difficulties in establishing accurate and complete figures, but the trend is quite unambiguous. The proportional decline has been continuous and uninterrupted, though the rate slowed dramatically in the peak protectionist years of 1929 to 1950. In absolute terms, of course, the numbers have increased because the world's population has increased so much, but even in absolute terms it is worth noting that the number of those living on a dollar a day (or less) was 1.16 billion in 1999, a significant decline, incidentally, from 1.3 billion in 1992. In 1820, the figure was about 0.9 billion. So the achievement of nearly two centuries of international capitalism is that there are about 260 million more people living in extreme poverty – but there are about 5,000 million more people who are at least better off than that.

How did it all begin? And does the global economic crisis which unfolded in 2007 mean that it is now about to end? A possible answer to the first question is that the British Industrial Revolution, which set off the modern phase of globalization around 1800, was made possible by technology, specifically the – then seemingly limitless – supplies of energy released by the systematic exploitation of fossil fuel. This, then, implies that the future of globalization depends on the future of world energy policy. Unless we can quickly come to rely only on renewable sources of energy, either climate change or the exhaustion of fossil fuels will cause the world economy and the world population to revert to their pre-nineteenth-century conditions, through natural disaster, disease, starvation or nuclear war. It is plainly the overriding task of the twenty-first century to avert such a catastrophe. However, it is not obvious that the problems of setting up a new world energy policy can be resolved independently of the problems thrown up by globalization, nor that an energy shortage or the consequences of climate change helped to precipitate the current worldwide economic crisis.

Nor is it clear that technological advances and the exploitation of coal will, on their own, explain why the British Industrial Revolution did not remain a local episode, without global implications. Findlay and O'Rourke point out that virtually all the technology that Western Europe had until the eighteenth century, including the use of coal for smelting, had existed earlier in China. In the course of the eleventh century, output from Chinese ironworks, eventually fuelled by coke, quadrupled, so that in 1078 China produced 150,000 tons of iron, equal to the entire European output of iron and steel in 1700. Kaifeng, its northern capital, had a population of 750,000, so was probably the largest city in the world, and the same size as London in the 1770s. Even in the late eighteenth century, the leading manufactured exports in the world were cotton textiles made in India and silk and porcelain made in China; and both China and India actually deindustrialized during the nineteenth century. There have been periods of rapid economic growth – of take-off, you might say – in various places and at various times in human history, but they have fizzled out, flopped back to earth – until Britain around 1800.

Findlay and O'Rourke do not believe there is a single causal explanation which will tell us why that particular take-off was sustained and generalized so as to affect, for better or worse, the whole world. But they draw attention to one factor of overwhelming importance – geography. What they think was crucial was the position of Western Europe, and especially of Britain, on the edge of the Atlantic, and so with unimpeded access, once command of the seas was achieved, to America. And America had one resource in abundance which in Britain and Europe generally was in strictly limited supply – land. Land was the source of not only living space but also food, fibre (wool and cotton), building materials and, until the industrial exploitation of coal, fuel too, in the form of wood. The West European economic spurt did not fizzle out, as all its predecessors had done, as a result of the constraints analysed by Malthus: population explosion leading to food shortages, leading, via starvation, to population collapse. And the reason it did not fizzle out was the land bank represented by the New World and the structure of international trade built upon it. 'This not only enabled Europe to import ever-increasing quantities of elastically supplied food and raw materials, but allowed it to send large numbers of people overseas at a time when its own population was growing rapidly'. A window of opportunity was opened which 'allowed Europe to pull decisively away from the Malthusian equilibrium', and permanent growth could take over from a stability imposed by the iron law of diminishing returns. European industrial manufacturing and American land were linked by international trade into a system which could grow throughout the nineteenth century – and which in the course of the nineteenth century was established on the North American continent, too: 'elastic overseas land supplies and declining transport costs were key factors . . . allowing Europe's population to grow at an expanding rate, without running into resource constraints, higher food prices, and lower living standards for the poor'. The Industrial Revolution and the nineteenth-century economic expansion of Europe were made possible by the ever-receding American frontier. By 1914, Europe and its offshoots, including America, controlled between them 84 per cent of the earth's surface. None of Africa-Eurasia's seven regions, not even Central Asia under Genghis Khan, had achieved anything remotely comparable before.

The year 1914 is, of course, an ominous date. It is the year when, there being nothing more to grab in the great outside, the members of the European region and its offshoots started to fight among themselves about the division of the spoils. World trade collapsed with the outbreak of war; protectionism, having helped to bring about the Great Depression, was in turn encouraged by it; and the period until 1945 can properly be called one of 'deglobalization'. The globalization that resumed, at first falteringly, after the Second World War, differed from the pre-1914 process in two important respects. First, it was largely confined, for the duration of the Soviet Empire and the Cold War, to America, Western Europe, Australasia, Southeast Asia and Japan. Capital transfers from the First World, to developing regions of the Third World, such as Africa and Latin America, were much lower in the late twentieth century than they had been in the late nineteenth. Inside the First World, after 1945, under American military protection and thanks to the stability provided by the Bretton Woods system of fixed exchange rates, trade prospered and capital accumulated, not only in the USA. However, the resultant need for a larger, more integrated and more international capital market, and for a rational pricing of the American military guarantee, caused the breakdown of fixed exchange rates from 1971 onwards, and in 1973 the sudden rise in oil prices at last transferred large amounts of First World capital into the Third. The potential for global banking was hugely extended, economic activity increased over a wider area, competition with the Second – communist – World intensified and, unable to satisfy its consumers while maintaining military parity, the Soviet bloc fell apart in 1989. The scale of economic globalization thereby once more became planetary, as it had not been since 1914; but the late nineteenth-century status quo was still not restored, and in these continuing differences lay the seeds of the crisis of 2007.

For, secondly, the globalization of economic life that we have seen over the last 30 years and that has done so much good, lifting hundreds of millions out of poverty and despair, has suffered from a dangerous one-sidedness. It has been a fully global process only in the abstract field of finance: restrictions on the trade of material goods have been more hesitantly removed, and the breakdown of the Doha round of negotiations has left many poverty-inducing tariffs and subsidies in place. For the majority of the world's population, manufacturing tariffs were higher in 2000 than they had been in 1913, and agricultural tariffs were no lower. In 2001, the total state assistance to farmers in rich countries – that is, principally North America, Europe and Japan – amounted to $311 billion, more than the GDP of sub-Saharan Africa. The World Bank estimates that if world trade in agriculture were liberalized – that is, if direct and indirect subsidies were abolished – the income of developing countries could by 2015 rise by $390 billion a year. Non-tariff barriers, such as quotas, were very much more significant at the end of the twentieth century than at the beginning. The most disruptive non-tariff barrier of all has been the continuing closure of national borders to economic migrants. While capital has been freed to move around the world with little hindrance, the movement of labour has, except within the European Union, been subjected to more stringent immigration controls. The late nineteenth century saw the biggest movements of population in human history, from Europe to America and across the British Empire, which (except for genocidal episodes, particularly in America and Australia) were largely peaceful and voluntary. But in the late twentieth century, the mismatch between economic globalization and local administrative protectionism has been manifest in the collision between a worldwide demand for free movement and the abuse of state power to prevent it. Surely a man should be able to travel as freely as a dollar? The freedom of neither need be absolute, but, since the one pays for the work of the other, the difference between them should not be so great as to amount to injustice. Justice Amin, at the age of 17, left his home in Ghana, where he had no prospects, to seek his fortune, like many real and fictional young men of the nineteenth century. As he laboured across Africa to the Libyan ports, the gateway to Europe, he marvelled at the billboards advertising BMWs and Wayne Rooney football gear: car sales and advertising franchises could cross the Mediterranean at the touch of a keyboard. He, however, was a human being, so his migration was illegal, and, like his travelling companions from all over West Africa, he had to make his journey in an unlicensed hulk (which sank and left him floating in a net for fishing tuna).

Money moves even more easily than BMWs. The expansion of the global financial market since the Second World War has, by contrast with the market in goods and labour, been explosive. Because restrictions on the movement of capital have been eliminated much more rapidly than those on anything more concrete, banking, perversely, has become the world's largest industry. By 2000, world output was something over five times what it had been in 1950, while international trade was sixteen times its 1950 level. There were not just more goods, but they were being traded much more. But the money required to trade them was changing hands very much more often – and, thanks to the computer, very much more quickly. Turnover in the foreign exchange markets around 1973, when the Bretton Woods system collapsed, was ten times the level of trade. In 2000, it was 50 times the level of trade, and by 2007 it was running at around $3 trillion a day, roughly 20 times the gross world product. Now money in the end is a promise to deliver in the future something other than money – the goods or services that it pays for – and the financial system is a miraculously ingenious mechanism for transforming a promise to deliver one thing in one place at one time into a promise to deliver something else in another place at another time. But it is possible to get carried away when making promises, and the little touch of over-optimism that individual promises may contain can be magnified by ingenuity into the collective construction of an implausible or impossible future. Over the last 30 years, some colossally implausible promises have been made. For most of that period, the long-term real interest rates greatly exceeded the growth rates of the G7 economies – so what was all the interest going to buy? The suspicion that generous promises might not in the end be honoured made the possession of something here and now more valuable – so asset prices rose. But, therefore, when money was borrowed on the assumption that the asset price would rise further, it was effectively borrowed on the assumption that the repayment of loans – the keeping of promises – was becoming increasingly unlikely. The tiger can survive only so long by eating his tail.

World trade grew hearteningly after 1989. But thanks to overleveraged financial derivatives, vastly too much was traded on the back of that increase in the trade in material goods and services. The imbalance between commercial and financial globalization was not only reflected in the continuing tariff disadvantages suffered by Third World economies. It also poisoned economic relations between the richest and most dynamic states. The inability to agree on a regulated system of world trade left some nations free to build up enormous trade surpluses, which they and their customers were willing to finance by equivalent mountains of debt (which global financiers then of course leveraged towards infinity). Domestic political imperatives made it much easier for the American government to postpone the reckoning and issue paper, rather than accept the economic restructuring that freer global trade required, while equivalent imperatives made the Chinese government willing to take the paper, rather than accept the political turmoil that would have followed the rise in consumption and the liberation of private capital had it allowed its currency to float. Governments have conspired with each other, against their peoples, to maintain their own power and freedom of action, in response to the threat of supranational regulation implicit in the growth of global trade and finance. But the illusion of their own omnipotence, which they have fostered, threatens to destabilize them, perhaps for good. Events have proved that Warren Buffett was right to identify derivatives such as credit default swaps as financial weapons of mass destruction, but the plutonium in them was supplied not by private enterprise but by governments. Derivatives increased the global supply of credit to the point where, in the event of a crisis, only the power of government could secure it, and the crisis duly arrived when the collapse of Lehman Brothers gave rise to the terrifying suspicion that credit had grown even further, to the point where it could not be secured even by the government of the USA. (The phrase 'the bank is too big to fail' really means 'the relevant government is too small to let it fail'.)

What is called the world financial crisis is in fact the beginning of a world political crisis. What went wrong with globalization after 1989 was not simply that the expansion of commerce remained too regulated and the expansion of finance too little. Rather, it was that, with the partial exception of the World Trade Organization, no regulation at all – political, military or economic – was established at the global level at which the human race was becoming interconnected and interdependent. This was particularly disappointing, since the new order set up in 1945 had been underpinned by a set of international bodies – especially the United Nations Organization, the International Monetary Fund and the World Bank – with a worldwide reach that had never been seen before (American participation marking a crucial difference between the UN and the League of Nations). These global institutions made for a vital political distinction between the world of 1945 and the world of 1914: they expressed an intention that the peaceful international competition and cooperation that it was hoped would follow on the end of world war should not end as late nineteenth-century globalization had ended – in irreconcilable conflict. But after 1989 they were not developed in that spirit but were treated with hostility or contempt – taken for granted, or dismissed as redundant, or blamed for external shocks, which national politicians did not want to admit were beyond their control. Even the most successful supranational institutions, those of the European Union, were misrepresented – during the discussions on a European constitution, for example – as the source of social and economic changes which originated outside Europe altogether in the global economy. There has been a failure at all levels, most fatefully at the level of politicians themselves, to grasp the simple truth that a global economy requires a global polity. The United Kingdom Independence Party (UKIP) denounced as absurd the existence of three EU directives on the loudness of lawnmowers: but why should that be more absurd than the existence of *sixteen* British Standards relating to the same subject? Internationally acknowledged standards are essential if there is to be international trade in industrial products at all, and one of the most admirable workers for global peace is the ISO, the International Organization for Standardization, in Geneva (which has itself produced four lawnmower standards, including an acoustic test-code). Global trade means global standards mean global regulation. But who is to regulate? For 20 years of boom after the fall of the Soviet Empire, that question went largely unasked in respect of the global financial system that makes global trade possible. The financiers, of course, thought it was enough to say that they could do the job themselves, and governments, sustained by the tax revenues banks were generating, did not want to raise the possibility that they might have to cede ownership of their milch cows to a collective farm. As a result, when the bust came, the governments could only lament that global banks could not be regulated, let alone underwritten, by national authorities. For the absence of global authorities with the necessary powers, however, they were themselves to blame. The lesson of 1914 was better learned by the generation of 1945 than by the generation of 1989.

The lesson of 1914 is still relevant today. Throughout the nineteenth century, for as long as the American frontier was open, it had not been necessary to pose the political question. Hegel remarked in the 1820s in his *Lectures on the Philosophy of World History* that until America reached its western geographical limits it could not achieve identity as a state. The moment in 1890 when the frontier was declared officially closed was a moment of profound, and more than symbolic, significance. The point of Hegel's remark had been that you cannot have identity as what he calls a state unless you are constrained in some way, unless you are limited by running out of resources, most basically of land. Politics is about how you decide to distribute things when there are not enough of them to go round, and your political character, your state identity, is determined by the decisions that you then take, decisions which will of necessity be unwelcome to some and imposed on them by force. The political significance of the closure of the frontier, of the declaration that from now on land was in limited supply, was not confined to the USA but affected the entire global system that depended on the prospect of indefinite expansion the frontier had afforded. For a quarter of a century after the carve-up agreed at the Berlin Conference of 1884–5, the scramble for Africa provided a substitute for America's wide-open spaces, but the political exigencies closed in: economic life was supranational, and it required a supranational political regulator to distribute the now limited resources. The imagination of the national and imperial governments of the time was not equal to such a challenge, and rather than meet it they marched into the killing fields of Flanders and Galicia. Perhaps, a century later, things have started to change for the better. The best reason for hoping that 2014 will not be like 1914, and that the stock market rout of 2007 will not, like those of 1907 and 1932, be followed seven years later by war, is that at the start of the twentieth century there were

37 intergovernmental organizations, and at the end of it there were 6,743. Whatever the great event that marks the end of the current crisis, and constitutes the next one, it will put in question the conventional ideas of nationhood and statehood that have marked the twentieth century. It may also change our perception of the nineteenth-century empires.

Chapter 3

Nations and Empires

The British Chancellor of the Exchequer was not the only one who failed to repair his roof while the sun was shining. The failure to extend economic globalization into the political realm during the years when cooperation should have been easy has left us with only dilapidated institutions in which to take shelter from the political consequences of the economic storm. National structures are too small to deal with global issues; international structures are too weak.

On the one hand, nation-states as they were thought to exist in the twentieth century, and perhaps also in the late nineteenth century, are plainly coming to an end, or have ended. International trade and travel, the movement of capital, goods, services and, to some extent, people, and the consequent international and political system of agreements and regulations covering everything from the labelling of foodstuffs to the commitment of troops and weapons for the common security, and the exchange of intelligence about the movements of individuals, have all developed to a point where it is not conceivable that a local state could reclaim authority over them without a radical deterioration in the conditions of life of its population. (Zimbabwe and Burma give examples of what happens when the attempt is nonetheless made.) On the other hand, the international state system under which we live today, the structure of physical force which provides the framework for the increasingly internationalized economic interaction of the world's population, is recent, experimental, manifestly unsatisfactory over large areas of the planet and possibly unstable as a whole.

I emphasize that the structure is recent. The theory is that the surface of the world and its human population are administered by a couple of hundred nation-states, each of which exercises the state monopoly of violence over a defined territory. Behind the theory lies a historical assumption that this political system is essentially a creation of the nineteenth century, and so largely coincident with the rise of the global economic system, as nations have sought to give their pre-existing cultural identity both political and economic expression in a world community of other similar actors. Both the historical assumption and the theory based on it seem to me false. Only at the end of the nineteenth century was it possible to conceive of the world's surface as subject in its entirety to some state or other, and by that time the foundations of our current economic order had long been in place. Moreover, the European and North American states to which most of this surface notionally belonged were not nation-states. What European country has ever been a nation-state pure and simple – Ireland, perhaps? But only because its claim is so recent. Before 1789 the concept is irrelevant, anyway. The main components of nineteenth-century Europe were federations, like Germany, or conglomerates of a metropolitan homeland and colonial dependencies, like France, or both at once, like Britain. In the twentieth century, it is true, the armistice period from 1919 to 1939 saw a number of experiments in local autonomy; but after 1945, sovereignty was pooled on both sides of the Iron Curtain, either in the Soviet Empire or in the developing European Union. Only as the destruction of the empires proceeded from 1918 to 1989 was it possible for the metropolitan states to advance, if that is the word, to the rank of nation-states, along with their former colonies. The territorial nation-state is in practice a twentieth-century invention. Its development is largely, and unsurprisingly, contemporaneous with the development of the structure of international agreements and international bodies which characterizes twentieth-century globalization. And many of the nation-states that have come into existence since 1945 have little more than their seat on these international bodies to demonstrate their statehood.

The one thing more that they all have, of course, is access to the instruments of violence. The disappearance of the nineteenth-century imperial states has left swathes of the earth's surface, above all in Africa, at the mercy of monopolists of physical force, who are nonetheless incapable of exercising the functions of a state over the territory notionally and often arbitrarily assigned to them: incapable of raising taxes or distributing benefits equally, of maintaining a legal system or guaranteeing property or a currency or their people from starvation, of preserving public order or grounding their own legitimacy in popular elections. These are not failed states, for usually there has never been a functioning local state power in the territory concerned. Rather, they are at best incipient states: a concentration of physical force that has yet to achieve the general acceptance that would make it an instrument of the people's will and so capable of sustaining an administration. At worst they are no better than the largest band of local brigands, possibly fighting it out with other aspirants in a civil war. These incipient state powers, however, are invested by the international system with sovereignty and legal personality and territorial integrity, with the right to receive aid monies and to purchase arms. The result, naturally enough, is corruption and crime on a very large scale. The dark underside of globalization, as

Ian Linden calls it,[*] is a consequence not of the growth
of a worldwide economic system but of our failure to
match it with a worldwide political system regulating the
deployment of physical force. That is why some of the
darkest corners of the present world order are to be found
in areas of sub-Saharan Africa and Latin America which
have hardly been touched by the growth in world trade.
In the absence of a credible state framework for economic
activity, Africa, with 10 per cent of the world's population,
attracts only 2 per cent of its foreign direct investment.
Africa, Linden comments, 'is not integrated into "the
global economy" in any meaningful sense'. If the present
political world order of territorial nation-states linked by
international agreements is, as I believe, an experiment
dating roughly from 1945, it is by no means obvious that
the experiment has yet succeeded, or will ever do so.

The theory on which the experiment is based is as
questionable as its historical presuppositions. For it is a
part of the definition of a nation as a political unit – in
which sense the term is synonymous with 'nation-state'
– that it asserts the right, and maintains the means, to
defend itself and its territory against other nations should
they become its enemies. You cannot be a nation on your
own: there have to be other nations from which you are

---

[*] Ian Linden, *A New Map of the World* (London: Darton, Longman and
Todd, 2003).

distinguished, which may become your enemies, and against which you can, if necessary, defend yourself. But that analysis cannot apply to a world in which one political unit, the United States of America, has the power, if it is prepared to pay the cost of using it, to unseat the government of any other political unit– not just Afghanistan or Iraq but also, in an extremity, its nearest nuclear rivals, Russia and China. That military disparity is only going to increase, and its political implications are fundamental. A world in which there is a hyperpower cannot be a world of nations: America cannot be a nation, because it has no equals; there is nothing else like it in the world, and you cannot be a nation on your own. America is still responsible for over 20 per cent of World Gross Product; in the first five years of the twenty-first century it contributed 36 per cent of the world's economic growth, more than twice as much as its nearest competitor, the European Union taken as a whole; and it spends something between 40 and 45 per cent of the world's entire military budget. Such a colossus cannot even have enemies, in the sense of other political units that, alone or in combination, can threaten its existence. A basic premise of the political theory of Carl Schmitt and Leo Strauss – that politics is about dealing with enemies – simply does not apply to it. Equally, no other political unit can share the world with America and still deserve the name of nation, since, however well armed it may be, it continues to exist only because America tolerates it. You cannot claim to be a self-determining people if America is the sleeping voter in any ballot you may hold on your collective future, and if the outcome is always subject to an American veto.

The fiction that the world is made up of self-determining sovereign nation-states, juridically equal, underlies what we still call international relations and the international bodies. The recognition, usually unacknowledged, that it is a fiction accounts both for America's occasional bouts of irritability in dealing with that international community and for the anti-Americanism of those who see America as the party-pooping rogue state. Most of what passes for anti-Americanism is a hostility, usually irrational, to the long process of globalization in which the USA happens for the present to be the leading actor, the vessel, as Hegel would put it, of the world spirit. The hostility is irrational since the global market grows only because, deep down, all those involved in it want it to grow, however much that deep desire may conflict with other, more superficial wishes. And as it grows it turns national boundaries and even national governments into obstacles to trade – which come increasingly to seem irrational, deserving to be circumvented where they cannot be abolished. It is the *international* domain which is nowadays the home of some of the most important structures that enable, condition and protect our collective lives: trade, capital, information, and for a significant and increasing number work itself; consumer goods provided, and even public services staffed and owned, by multinational companies; and military forces equipped by foreign powers and largely deployable only in concert with them. How weak nonetheless are the strictly governmental functions at the international level – the maintenance of peace, and of the integrity of the medium of exchange, and the prevention of starvation – the history of the last 20 years shows only too well.

But surely nations are the flavour of the century? Never have there been so many, or so small: Palau, one of the smallest of all the 192 members of the United Nations, has around 20,000 inhabitants. Why is the concept of nation-hood so lively, so current and so troublemaking, *despite* the fact that so much of what is important in people's lives comes to them, and is known by them to come to them, from outside the bounds of a nation? Part of the answer is that nations matter to us in the global market *because* they are comfortable, convenient, deceptive self-images. The concept of 'my nation' gives a human face not just to my nostalgia (if I think of my nation as old) or my idealism (if I think of it as still in the making) but also to my anger and hatred when some external or supra-national power – America, or the EU – seems to threaten its identity, my identity. My nation matters to me because it is a defence which stands between me and what I fear. And what I fear is the truth of my condition: that I am an atom and much of my life is dependent on processes of a complexity I cannot understand, involving inconceivable numbers of people I can never know, in places I shall never see. Nations are now the user-friendly interfaces between the individual consumer-producer and the global market. The computing analogy is both apposite and exact. It is apposite because computing is in many ways the instrument through which globalization is driven forward – the technical means by which current volumes of transnational trade and finance are made possible, and the medium in which a truly global unity is created, all information being in principle available at the same time and in one place, on the screen. But the analogy is also exact: the nation is exactly like a computing interface, which adapts for different individual users' convenience and comfort the underlying and to most of us completely incomprehensible codes and processes which are what we are really using when we download a file or send an email. That underlying system is common to all communicating machines, however different the interfaces that present themselves to the different users, and the repertoire of different interfaces is itself a feature of the underlying system. The computer pretends to speak our language, but in fact it speaks its own universal code. The nation pretends to be what gives us life, substance and identity, but in fact we are increasingly dependent on, and even made by, the global economic order, the dictates of which are passed on to us, brewed under licence, so to speak, by HM Government or some other UK subsidiary.

Once upon a time, nothing defined a nation so effectively and unquestionably as its language. Language, Wittgenstein assured us, was a form of life. Like a life, language was at the same time unique and infinite – it was a unique way of experiencing and articulating absolutely everything. For that reason it was worth studying another language, for nothing could ever substitute for it as a means of sharing and understanding the experience of others. One of the most puzzling cultural features of the last 20 years is the decline of interest in foreign languages at a time when life has in so many respects become so international. (The phenomenon is also noticeable in non-Anglophone countries in respect of languages other than English.) The conventional explanation is that economic globalization has gone along with the advance of English to the status of global language. I think, though, that the explanation is different, for the real global language is not English but the operating code of computers. And as more and more of our communication takes place through computers, or has to be in a form that is at least manipulable by computers, so languages become increasingly reduced to optional interfaces between users of the same universal code. There is less incentive to learn foreign languages to talk to sceptical foreign bank clerks when the hole-in-the-wall cash machines in Prague and

Barcelona both display as their first message the choice of languages in which you can give and receive your instructions. Microsoft regularly makes new issues of its software available in upward of 35 languages. Language in this sense is no longer an ultimate determinant of an identity its users cannot escape but an optional style – what we can't escape in the global market is Microsoft.

What is happening to languages is happening to the nations that in the nineteenth century (but not before then) languages defined. The global network does not make languages or nations obsolete; on the contrary, it preserves them. They are useful and comfortable points of contact between the global system and the individual. Nations and languages survive, indeed become the object of fierce and explicit loyalty, like football teams, but they have been instrumentalized; they are the medium and channel for something else, something that more deeply gives us what we want and makes us what we are. Nations won't go away. But equally they won't give us what we promise ourselves from belonging to them. We mustn't let ourselves be fooled into thinking that investigating national differences, or even tensions between nations, is going to tell us much about the reality of our present situation or our likely future after the Great Event.

We need instead to focus our minds on the reality of 'international' relations, both in the past and in the present, and that reality is imperial. The basic building blocks of the international order have consistently been not nations but empires.

At least in the period since the European commercial revolution began in the thirteenth century, the function of empire has been to provide political, that is, non-market-based and so ultimately military, protection for the structures of the developing global market over as much as possible of the territory to which at any time the market extends. As soon as trade, or any other form of economic or cultural interaction between members of different political units begins, a higher-order political authority is called for to guarantee the conditions of the interaction: the security of the communications, the enforceability of the agreements, the integrity of the common currency. The political units may be no more than towns, but the higher-order authority to which they submit, voluntarily or under compulsion, will have the character and deserve the name of empire. That was already the case in the earliest years of the commercial revolution when the Holy Roman Empire of the German Nation struggled to hold together the territories south and north of the Alps in which the new economy was being born – the merchants and bankers of the North Italian city-states and the silver mines of Central Europe which provided them with their bullion. The global reach both of the economic system and of the political structure needed to secure it was already manifest in the empire of

Charles V, the first on which it was truly said that the sun never set. Niall Ferguson, in his study of what he believes to be the American empire,[*] has shown most convincingly that no politico-military structure in the history of our planet has been a more effective patron of globalization, and in particular of the transfer of capital to the developing areas of the world, than the British Empire of the nineteenth and early twentieth centuries. However, the domestic economic power base of the British Empire was not sufficiently in advance of its competitors – indeed it was, notoriously, falling behind that of Germany – and its military guarantee lost credibility as a result. Even at its height, the British Empire was not adequate to the task of being protector and guarantor of an economy that, at the latest by 1885, was consciously global. The inability of the Great Powers to identify, or invent, such a guarantor was the fundamental cause of the Seventy-Five Years' War from 1914 to 1989, in the course of which the rival imperial structures inherited from the nineteenth century gradually destroyed one another. The empires that remained – China, the Russian Federation shorn of its Asian and European colonies, and the continental United States – were all territorially compact polities which could masquerade as nation-states exercising a monopoly of

---

[*] Niall Ferguson, *Colossus: The Rise and Fall of the American Empire* (London: Allen Lane, 2004).

force over a defined geographical area. Their internal structure, the imperial relationship between their central authorities and their constituent political units, required nothing like the integration into the still expanding global economic system that had been fundamental to the great trading empires of the previous century, above all the British. For all three of them autarky and isolationism seemed conceivable political options, provided the underlying centuries-old logic of globalization was ignored and the extent to which their prosperity, or their hope for it, was dependent on their involvement in the global economy.

But of course globalization cannot be ignored. The crisis that began in 2007 has at least the merit of demonstrating beyond question the interdependence even of the economic giants of the twenty-first century. It has also demonstrated the absence of a conceptual and institutional framework capable of representing and regulating their relations with each other and the more fragmented world of Latin America, Africa, the Middle East and Southeast Asia, or the relations of these powers among themselves. The dogmatic presumption that the world is or ought to be made up of nation-states in which society, economy and state are coterminous not only prevents recognition of imperial relations within polities, or of their underlying economic connections, but also obscures from view the power relations between them

that will be of crucial importance in the new political settlement – violent or otherwise – in which the crisis must
eventually terminate. Russia's difficulties with Chechnya
or Georgia or Chinese immigration across the Amur,
China's difficulties with Tibet or Taiwan or its Islamic
minorities, or the USA's with Panama or Haiti or Cuba,
the EU's embarrassment with the Balkans or (one day)
with Kaliningrad, or Turkey's or Iraq's with the Kurds cannot be resolved by deciding (and who decides?) which is
here the nation or what is its territory. These are matters
of 'spheres of influence' – as Russia remarked with com-
mendable clarity in its Georgian war, reverting to a phrase
from the imperial era. 'Regional hegemons' do not have
the juridical status of empires, but their existence reveals
a transnational dimension of political life that empires
once occupied. It will be occupied again, whether the
second decade of the century brings an economic and
environmental disaster or the collaboration necessary
to prevent it. Rising tides and temperatures, advancing
deserts or ice caps (if the Gulf Stream switches off) do not
stop at national borders, nor, as we have already seen, does
freely moving capital in a regime of floating exchange
rates. The inadequacy of the concept of the nation-state
to the issues that face us is most crassly evident in the case
of Israel. A 'two-state solution' to the problems of Jewish–
Palestinian relations is manifestly impossible: whatever an
autonomous Palestinian region might be, it could not be

a state; for how could Israel allow it the military capability it would need to establish itself as the local monopolist of force – to defend itself, for example, against Israeli intrusion? And how could two such unequal parties agree on the equitable distribution of a diminishing resource vital to both of them: the water of the Jordan River? So one state it will have to be – except that any constitution accommodating both hostile interests would require such internal fragmentation of territory and competences, and an external guarantor with such powers of adjudication, that the result, once again, could not be called either a unitary or an independent state.

But because the nation-state model is so recently established and so shallowly rooted – essentially it is no older than modern Israel itself – global governance may be nearer than we think. States will certainly continue, but there is no reason to assume that they will be nation-states, laying claim to complete control of their populations or their territory. More and more of their activities will be shared, either with other states or with international or supranational bodies. If as a consequence of the crisis of 2007 America's relative economic strength declines and the mismatch grows between its share of World Gross Product and its continuing military dominance, the world hegemon will have to rethink its role.

Since the end of the Seventy-Five Years' War in 1989, American military power and the American dollar, though presented and largely understood as national institutions, have deputized for the imperial guarantees of security and financial stability that the global market has needed. At a time when the bulk of the world's economic transactions took place between 10 to 15 per cent of its population, and something between a half and a third of that population was in the USA anyway, this was a reasonably effective substitute for an empire. But as China, India, Brazil and Russia join the world economy, so the day becomes more foreseeable when half the human beings on the planet will be significant agents in a market that only a truly imperial authority can regulate. The only conceivable peaceful route to that goal is through a continuation of the *pax Americana*, but both the world's understanding of America and America's understanding of itself would have to change fundamentally for the goal to be achieved.

If we ask where the obsolescent fiction originates that the world consists of self-determining nations, the answer is of course the USA. The self-determination of nations sounds like one of those principles so self-evident as to be timeless, if not tautological, but, though it was already being invoked in the late nineteenth century, it played no decisive role in world affairs until Woodrow Wilson made it a central element in his 14-point plan for reconstruction after 1918. It is essentially an American invention. It quickly served its initial function of dismembering the

German-language empires of Europe, which no doubt pleased the relevant expatriates in the USA. But German observers at least could see that it would soon corrode the imperial structures of the victor powers too, and this also may have been part of the American intention: the dismantling of the Empire was one of the essential conditions for setting up the lend-lease agreements by which America financed the British war effort of 1939–45. In Wilson's vision, the League of Nations complemented the principle of self-determination, even though he could not persuade his countrymen to sign up for it; and its more fortunate successor, the United Nations, almost equally an American invention, also reposes on that principle. Both bodies may look on the surface like attempts to bring the human race together. Beneath the surface, however, they have an opposite intention and, indeed, to some extent an opposite effect. They both, at the time of their inception, incorporated a refusal to recognize the then real economic and political structures holding the human race together, namely, the colonial empires. And they both presupposed that the building blocks of the world order, the political units of which the human race was composed, were nations. Both bodies united only what they had first divided. And what did they divide the human race into? Replicas of the original self-determining nation, America.

The USA has had a complex and troubled relationship

with the ideas of nationhood and statehood, and the future security of the world may depend on its ability to show once again its astonishing powers of self-renewal.

Chapter 4

The Religion of America

The coming renegotiation of the international settlement of 1945 will require a new definition – explicit or implied – of what it is to be a state in relation with other states. The fiction that there can be such things as self-determining nation-states will have to be abandoned. It will be essential that, as the most considerable locus of physical force in the world, the USA shares fully in that redefinition, which will be a redefinition of itself. For the USA has long seen itself as in a double sense a self-determining nation. In the first place, its population is almost entirely composed of immigrants and the descendants of immigrants, and, as far as the non-African element is concerned, the immigration was almost entirely voluntary. In that, the USA is not unique, though the scale of the population movement involved and its continuation over four centuries are surely without parallel. The USA is an extraordinary monument to the human power of choice. It is a human landscape built, as no other is, by the conscious decisions of those who make it up. In the life of the head of every migrant family, whether their migration brought them success or destitution, there was a moment when they put their trust in the most fundamental form of the principle underlying the free market: we choose not just what we have but who we are. In order to be a European you merely have to accept your fate, whether you understand that as your personal past, your family or social tradition or your fashioning by your physical surroundings. You don't have to move. You don't even have to think about the matter. Behind every white American lies, in the recent or distant past, a moment when someone made a free choice of something different.

And there's the rub. The free choice of self-creation comes at a price, as the young Hegel demonstrated with overwhelming brilliance in his analysis of the archetypal migrant, Abraham. Abraham turned his back on the concrete complexity of the urban society of Ur of the Chaldees to follow a summons as singular, abstract and featureless as his own self, and went out into a desert that mirrored it. The choice for freedom is a choice against all the determinations that the migrant leaves behind. The choice for America was a choice against Europe, and the early colonists easily conceived their destination as the Land Promised to Abraham and Moses, for the sake of which they were abandoning Ur and Egypt. When in

1630 John Winthrop, the first Governor of Massachusetts, preached on the *Arbella* the sermon in which he likened the colony he and his fellow emigrants were setting out to found to a 'city on a hill', he concluded by adapting the words of Moses in Deut. 30.18 so that the Atlantic Ocean stood in for the River Jordan:

> If . . . *wee shall be seduced and worshipp and serve other Gods,* our pleasure and proffitts . . . it is propounded unto us this day, *wee shall surely perishe out of the good land whither we passe over this vast sea to possesse it.*

Winthrop's own Puritanism was relatively moderate, but there will have been many in his company who could draw from the biblical analogy the severest conclusions about the old England they were leaving for the new:

> And so, as the first calling of the Gentiles after Christ came, was accompanied with a rejection of the Jews, so the first calling of the Jews to be God's people, when they were called out of Egypt, was accompanied with a rejection of the Gentiles

wrote Jonathan Edwards, the reviver of that original severity, a century later. The exodus from Egypt and the passage of the Red Sea were images of the calling of God's elect from a life of sin and their conversion to righteousness. If they also served as images of the voyage to Massachusetts, then the implications for the papistical Anglicanism of the court of Charles I were clear enough. America's self-determination was a rejection of the religion of Europe.

In time it eventually became a religion of the rejection of Europe. The second sense in which the USA has thought of itself as a self-determining nation dates from 1776. The first Industrial Revolution was well under way, the seemingly limitless resources of the North American land bank guaranteed that it would not fizzle out and the British imperial system was beginning to take on its nineteenth-century form. However, the system still lacked a fully global military reach, and in the mid-eighteenth century the North American planters chafed under its restrictions. The more active of them wanted 'trade with all parts of the world', whether in tea, sugar or slaves, and they wanted to expand their domestic market westward into the Indian territories, which the imperial authorities were still endeavouring to protect. But even those gentlemen farmers, like Washington or Jefferson, who saw the future only as an indefinite multiplication of themselves, extending the benefits of landownership to all economic agents, large and small, silently presupposed an endless supply of land opened up by the frontier's endless westward advance. The moment when the United Colonies chose to follow the imperative to undefined economic expansion rather than accept the limitations imposed by an imperial authority that sought to balance their interests with those of others was the moment when they chose an identity for America as the instrument of globalization. They rejected the indirect route to the world market offered by the patronage of a European empire and, dissenting from Europe's political economy as their ancestors had dissented from its religion, struck out on their own. But there is a fundamental contradiction between wanting to be on your own and wanting to be for the world, between being a nation and being for the global marketplace, and the contradiction was noted in Britain.

It was not merely the appeal of a debating point that in 1775 led Samuel Johnson to ask at the end of his pamphlet 'Taxation No Tyranny', 'how is it that we hear the loudest yelps for liberty among the drivers of negroes?' The question emerged directly from his polemic against the apologies for rebellion then beginning to be issued by the Philadelphia Congress. For the American Whigs, such as Jefferson, all social arrangements between human beings were agreements between freely contracting parties seeking mutual benefits, the model being agreements for the sale and purchase of goods and services. Society was in its essence civil society, as Hegel calls it, the sum of those institutions which individuals and their families find convenient for transacting the business of what Hegel also calls the system of needs and their satisfaction. The land any family might require for simple subsistence was freely available and there was no reason why such a society, built on consensual arrangements for mutual or even general advantage, should not be extended to all who wished to take part in it, on the American continent or anywhere round the world. Any pretension of the British or any other crown or empire to limit, direct or tax those transactions, or indeed the ownership of land, was in principle illegitimate. However, the mere existence of the institution of slavery – even regardless of its economic importance to Jefferson's society – was the clearest possible demonstration of the inadequacy of this view. For since few slaves, if any, had willingly agreed to become the property of another it was evident that there was more to the institution of property than the mutual consent of vendor and purchaser. There was also the power of compulsion: not just the power of force by which land might be wrested from its aboriginal inhabitants but the power by which whatever was sold was secured as the property of the purchaser against the will of anyone who wished to deprive him of it – in the extreme case of slavery, against the will of the person bought. The burden of Johnson's critique of the Philadelphians was that they owed – they necessarily owed – 'their political existence . . . the solemnities of legislation, the administration of justice, the security of property' not to a free agreement to associate but to the power of government, in their case to the royal grant of their charters. To the argument that 'Liberty is the birthright of man, and where obedience is compelled, there is no liberty', Johnson retorted the 'equally simple' answer: 'Government is necessary to man, and where obedience is not compelled, there is no government.' Johnson was associating himself with a tradition of political thought which runs from Hobbes through Hegel to Weber for which society cannot be understood to result solely from the free choices of the marketplace but must be seen to include the actions of the state, the monopoly owner of the power to coerce. 'There must', he writes, 'in every society, be some power or other, from which there is no appeal . . . It is not infallible, for it may do wrong; but it is irresistible, for it can be resisted only by rebellion, by an act which makes it questionable, what shall be thenceforward the supreme power'.

Jefferson would not acknowledge that what was at issue in the struggle that finally began in the year after Johnson's pamphlet was the question of what was thenceforward to be the supreme power among the United Colonies. Indeed, his words inaugurating the struggle do their best to conceal the point altogether. The rhetorical embellishments with which he surrounded the bald sentences of Lee's Resolution for Independence of 7 June 1776 were a *post-factum* justification for a decision already taken, and stronger in such religious sentiments as a deist could muster than in the analysis of political theory or practice. That, after all, was what the occasion required, and Jefferson rose to it magniloquently. The embarrassment that most of the measures held by the colonists to be oppressive had been imposed by a parliamentary legislature whose members had principles largely similar to their own was overcome by devoting well over half of the Declaration to 23 grievances represented as the personal responsibility of the British King. The enemy from whom independence was declared was three times identified as the enemy in principle of self-determination: 'absolute tyranny' and 'absolute rule'. Now George III undoubtedly wanted to be more of an autocrat than parliament would allow him to be, but to assimilate his constitutional position to that of Louis XVI or Frederick the Great suggests a certain detachment from reality. But reality is not what Jefferson's Declaration was about. The Declaration was concerned, rather, to obscure the origins of secession in economic and political tensions between the constituent parts of the nascent British Empire. It aimed instead to represent secession in the religious terms in which the founders of the colonies had explained to themselves their choice of something different: the willed separation of the righteous from the life of wickedness in the Old World by their passage through the baptismal waters of the Atlantic under the guidance of Divine Providence. America, Jefferson made his fellow representatives declare, must 'totally dissolve' all connection with the evil empire of transatlantic absolutism, embodied in the improbably satanic figure of the British monarch, and embark on the new life of 'Free and Independent States' in accordance with the 'Laws of Nature and of Nature's God'. The political theology of the Declaration is characteristic of its author, perhaps fatefully so. For Jefferson could never reconcile himself to what was self-evident to Johnson: the constitutive role of the state, the monopoly deployment of force in the collective interest, specifically for the control or limitation of markets. The United Colonies could not, of course, found a free and independent identity without appropriating to themselves the power of coercion. The Declaration certainly envis-ages the existence of such a power in what it says about the future foreign relations of the colonies, which will be entitled to 'levy war, conclude peace, contract alliances' and so on. But of the internal domestic role of that power, in determining who this new actor on the world stage will be, the Declaration says only that it will not be exercised by Great Britain. Nothing whatever is said about how the coercive political authority confiscated from Britain will be applied to establish over what territories the new entity will extend, who its members will be or the right by which those who make the Declaration may claim to represent them (after all, a significant proportion of the colonies' inhabitants disagreed with what was said and done at Philadelphia). Rather than base the identity of the new America on any political structure, representative or otherwise, the authority of which would ultimately repose on force, Jefferson bases it on rights. And rather than acknowledge that rights imply enforcers, too, and a right that is not justiciable is meaningless, Jefferson bases his rights on someone who otherwise plays very little role in his thinking – God. Jefferson appeals to God as politicians, not only American, have done ever since: in order to conceal something that they do not wish to call by its name, whether their violent intentions or only their incompetence or powerlessness. Jefferson does not want to admit the role of compulsion, rather than choice, in determining what a nation is, and, specifically, what America is. He covers it, therefore, with what remains to him of the theological vocabulary through which his Puritan immigrant predecessors assimilated their self-determination to an inscrutable Divine election. America is to become a free and independent nation through the exercise of God-given unalienable rights, not – as in fact of course happened – through the establishment of an autonomous local monopoly of force, an American state. Over a conceptual elision the Declaration of Independence casts a cloak of religious oratory. From beneath the cloak only that use of force required by the rejection of the European mother country is allowed to protrude.

The religion of America has grown over the centuries, acquiring its liturgies and feast days, its saints and its cultic objects, such as the flag (the veneration of which, by the way, clearly contradicts the First Amendment). It has also acquired a magnificent set of temples in Washington, including the Jefferson Memorial, on the walls of which sentences from the religion's founding scripture are incised in letters a yard high. Anti-Europeanism and anti-imperialism are almost as intrinsic to this religion as Jefferson's conceptual elision, but only intermittently has the anti-Europeanism been as apparent as it is in Jefferson's remark of 1816 to John Adams:

> Old Europe will have to lean on our shoulders, and to hobble along by our side, under the monkish trammels of priests and kings, as she can. What a colossus shall we be [. . .]

Old Europe's kings, note, are as monkish as its priests: the European political order is dismissed with the gesture of a Pilgrim Father turning from Europe's papistical religion, while the new American order that outgrows it takes on the aura of a religious alternative by its association with the Rhodian statue of Apollo. That the new colossus will necessarily be as imperial as any of the old European empires is not remarked on.

The conceptual elision itself, however, has remained a permanent obstacle to America's self-understanding. The struggle against it reached a first culmination in the Constitution of 1787, a genuinely world-historical act of

self-definition, but a rearguard action by the Jeffersonians
dealt the Constitution a disabling blow by appending to
it the so-called Bill of Rights. The first ten amendments
reinstalled near the heart of American identity the political theology of the Declaration and its elision of the true
nature of the state. The remarkable, and unprecedented,
feature of the Constitution of 1787 was its definition,
through the unanimous agreement on a form of words,
of a supreme power, the creation of a government. A bill
of rights, however, Jefferson wrote to Madison, 'is what the
people are entitled to against every government on earth',
and in the first ten amendments to the Constitution a
sustained attempt was made to obliterate its achievement
by concealing the concept of government and subordin-
ating it to that of 'the people'. In the Constitution proper
the people are, I think, mentioned only twice: first, in the
preamble, as the people of the United States who ordain
and establish the Constitution; and second in Section 2.1
of Article 1, as the body of electors to the House of
Representatives in the several states. In both cases they
are territorially defined and are envisaged as the source of
all the powers which the document establishes or delim-
its. In the Bill of Rights, however, a considerably shorter
text, 'the people' are referred to five times, three times
in the phrase 'the right of the people'; they are nowhere
territorially defined; and they are envisaged throughout
as the possessors of rights or powers distinct from those

of the government of the United States and from those enumerated in the Constitution. How the number, nature or extent of these extra-constitutional rights and powers is to be determined, in what they originate, or how they are to be defended against the supreme power (including the Supreme Court) which the Constitution establishes, is not stated. In the Constitution the people have no rights because they set up the government, which defines and defends all rights. In the first ten amendments the people have become a pre-political and pre-legal society of indefinite geographical extent, with pre-original rights and powers which can have come only from Nature and Nature's God. In the Bill of Rights, as in the Declaration of 1776, concepts that are ultimately religious in origin are used to conceal that the supreme power of the new American state has to be irresistible like any other because to resist it is rebellion, setting up another supreme power in its place.

That Johnson, not Jefferson, was right about the new America was shown by the course of history. That the American state was no different from any other, that its fundamental right was its might, became bitterly apparent to the defeated party in the Civil War. The Confederacy, misled by the omission of the political facts of life from the Union's founding myth, took at face value its hymn to self-determination and choice, assumed it had the same unalienable right to independence as Jefferson's

generation and suffered the usual fate of foolish virgins.
But among the victors the conceptual elision continued
– it had, after all, served them well. The huge industrial
expansion that followed the Civil War, and the renewal
of the original drive to the west that had precipitated the
declaration of 1776, reinforced the old illusion that a
specifically American identity could be found in the forces
that were making for a global economic system – in the
system of needs and their satisfaction – rather than in the
non-economic force of coercion deployed by a state.

But in the darkness beneath Jefferson's cloak, as
Johnson knew, and brutally told what he knew, a bad conscience has festered. For if behind every white American
lies someone's act of self-determination, behind every
black American lies someone's act of violent enslavement.
(As the descendant of voluntary immigrants, President
Obama belongs, in this sense, to the white community.)
Every black face in America is a reminder of the truth that
the Declaration of Independence conceals – that human
societies are constituted not only by choice but also by
force, not only by the market but also by the state. Black
America reminds white America that it is not a miraculous
exception to the laws of history, a free association based
on an original shared recognition of God-given rights,
but a state based on an original, and continuing, asser-
tion of irresistible power – and so reminds white America
also of the conceptual elision by which it has forgotten

its origins. Moralizing breast-beating – the shamefaced admission that America sinned against its founding principles in permitting slavery – is a defence mechanism which permits the elision to continue and the political truth to remain unrecognized – that the political association of Americans, as of anyone else, is founded not on principles but on force. This defence has another advantage: it makes it possible to claim that the sin was expiated in the bloodletting of the Civil War (understood as a war of principle, against the slavery of Black Americans), so that the event which ought to demonstrate definitively the true nature of the American Union can become a further instrument for concealing it. But Black America remains as an unsettling reminder, not that America once offended against Jefferson but that Jefferson was wrong.

Jefferson, however, is, at the very least, a saint of the American religion. If a saint tells you that there is no elephant in the drawing room – and the American state, founded on force, looks remarkably like an elephant – you have, as a believer, two possible courses of action. You can, like the inheritors of the Northern party in America's ultimately defining conflict, agree not to mention the elephant, elide reality and accept living with an uneasy conscience as the price you pay for the fruits of victory. Or, like the inheritors of the Southern defeat, you can decide to call the elephant something else. Rather than admit that your world has been remade by a power that the victors do not allow you to name, you can invoke against them the God they themselves make use of to conceal the truth about their origins. The belief that America was made by God, not by the Yankee state, however heretical and indeed implausible that belief may be, appeals to older and more powerful emotions than the deism of the Declaration of Independence. Harold Bloom[*] discerned the real issue in the American debate about the teaching of creationism in schools: not the defence of any theological doctrine but a desperate emotional need that the reality and solidity of the Bible should be recognized, almost regardless of what the Bible may be held to say, the need that the Bible should be *there*, like a rock, or a mountain. Bloom did not, however, appreciate the political significance of the emotional need. The longing that the ethical substance of life should be concretely present to all can be fulfilled, according to Hegel, only in the state, and any surrogate for the state, political or religious, is necessarily inadequate. Understandably, the Northern Unionists, the East and West Coast liberals, tremble when a seventeenth-century God arises in the Bible Belt and His trumpetings start to shatter the teacups. But that God is no more (and no less) an illusion than the constitutional fiction of God-given rights and principles by which they

---

[*] Harold Bloom, *The American Religion: The Emergence of The Post-Christian Nation* (New York: Simon and Schuster, 1993).

live in the North. The North has its bad conscience, and the South has its Bible. But neither God is the real name of the elephant. The real, but hidden, God of the American religion is the irresistible American state.

Most countries have myth-like conceptions of their own past, often involving religion and often fostered by the attempt to understand themselves as nation-states. Lithuania has almost as many illusions about its historical relations with Christianity and with Poland as England has about Scotland, Ireland, Protestantism and the Empire – all summed up in its uncertainty about whether its population is English or British. But Lithuania and England are not the hyperpower. America's myth matters to the world because it conditions the hyperpower's understanding both of its relation with other states and of the changing world order. On 11 April 2003, Donald Rumsfeld justified America's refusal to keep its obligation, under the Geneva Convention, to maintain law and order in the Iraq it had just occupied, saying that 'Free people are free to make mistakes and commit crimes and do bad things'. These wickedly complacent words came from, and appealed to, a native intellectual tradition that cannot recognize that freedoms exist only in so far as collectively willed force prevents their violation and that the market, the realm of choice, and the state, the realm of compulsion, are mutually dependent. It is unfortunately improbable that Iraq will prove the graveyard of that tradition. The hugely wealthy Liberty Fund, for example, will no doubt continue its discrete operations, paying academics and opinion-formers to promulgate the American religion even though its doctrines have been comprehensively discredited. But the event that will decide the character of the twenty-first century will be America's decision, in the face of global crisis, to maintain or abandon its belief in its own divine exceptionality.

Chapter 5

Living with the Elephant

When Hegel pronounced that America could not achieve identity as a state until it reached its geographical limits and no longer had a permanently receding western frontier, he did not appreciate that even when he spoke America had already settled for the partial identity of an unacknowledged state, which it would retain long after its territorial limits had been fixed. Nor did he appreciate that America would impose this partial identity on nations at large, would promote their own illusion of self-determining independence and would refuse to acknowledge the necessity of political, military and imperial bonds between them – while it would nonetheless in practice have to run an empire like any previous hegemon. Since the moment of decision in 1776, the USA and, latterly, the whole world have had to live with the consequences of America's unwillingness to integrate its original commitment to indefinite economic expansion with the limiting and disciplining power of the state, represented by the federal armed forces.

Internally, the unwillingness to integrate is manifest, for example, in gun laws, based on a reluctance to acknowledge the state's monopoly of force; in the recourse to state power through litigation, unrestricted by a concept of public interest, rather than through legislation; and in the denial to the state of the means of self-perpetuation through the refusal to require it to maintain a complete register of electors. The society that results can seem to those who inhabit it a place of personal liberty, physical self-respect, equality before the law and confidence that the collective life is the choice of all its members who choose to choose. Or it can seem a place of permanent insecurity, where physical violence and legal challenge always threaten, where public goods are treated with suspicion and where poverty spells exclusion from the political as well as the economic system. These unreconciled perspectives clearly mark the American bureaucracy which, uniquely in the world, combines the self-righteousness of the instrument of government of the people by the people for the people with the resentful awareness that the people's political theology treats it as an unwelcome intrusion on their rights. As a result, like the victim of some inferiority complex, it bears down principally on those who cannot afford the professional assistance to keep it at bay, on non-citizens and on the disenfranchised poor.

Externally, the unresolved conflict within the American identity reproduces itself in a parallel uncertainty. Does America's claim to nationhood require a willingness to deal with other nations on equal terms, and to bind itself by international agreements and entry into international bodies? Or does the intrinsic boundlessness of the American economic idea, its foundational commitment to the global market, currently manifest in its economic power and consequential military might, and in a sense legitimized by them, imply the underlying illegitimacy, the immorality, of all other state structures that call themselves nations but, unlike America, acknowledge their foundation in their local monopoly of force? This uncertainty has its mirror image in the non-American mind: should America be welcomed as the bearer of global economic integration and prosperity beyond national boundaries, or should it be feared as the bully among the nations? Should economic and cultural globalization be welcomed as releasing the potential of us all to be citizens of the world? Or should it be feared as the instrument of American national self-interest? Should the omnipresence and unlimited operational autonomy of the American military be welcomed as the only practicable way in which a hyperpower can commit itself to maintaining international order? Or should it be feared as the expression and weapon of a will to nationhood which will one day plunge the world into nuclear war rather than accept the relative national decline that globalization must bring? Both as it appears internally to its own citizens and as it appears externally to others, American identity is shrouded in ambiguity and what Joseph S. Nye[*] and Niall Ferguson have called paradox. American identity remains only partial, and only partially conscious, because of the suppression by America's founders of the role of state power in defining their independence and their substitution for it of supposedly self-evident God-given rights.

Religion – whether the personal religion of Americans or the public religion of America – is therefore an essential constituent of this partial identity, the instrument of the conceptual elision, the means by which the repression of reality is maintained. When George W. Bush told the Palestinian foreign minister that God told him to invade Afghanistan and Iraq, he was preventing the discussion from touching on considerations of American interests, or power, or position in a global system. Jefferson's declaration that America was being founded in accordance with the laws, not of men but of God, is still maintained in order to prevent scrutiny of what America is, does or intends – and that aversion from the real, sometimes called 'idealism', was intrinsic to America's first and second acts of self-determination. For that reason, it is

---

[*] Joseph S. Nye, *The Paradox of American Power: Why the World's Only Superpower Can't Go It Alone* (Oxford: Oxford University Press, 2002).

a very strange thing, perhaps even an impossibility, to be an American who does not believe in God, and the extraordinary importance of the issues of abortion and homosexuality in recent American politics is surely due to the power those issues have to characterize certain views, first as irreligious and then, in consequence, as un-American. It is not the superstition, literal-mindedness or assisted suicide of the intellect that most grates on European observers of American biblical fundamentalism but the, possibly obscure, awareness that they are witnessing a compulsive repetition of America's original declaration of independence, a reiteration of the *proton pseudos*, the original refusal of self-knowledge, on which American identity is based.

In the home life of the American psyche, Jefferson's conceptual elision persists as what is thought of as the frontier mentality: Mrs Palin's belief that it is possible at the same time to shoot moose in Alaska and to occupy the Chief Executive's Office in the Washington HQ of the military hyperpower. Even though the frontier closed over a century ago, the belief that somewhere it was still open, that the land that fuelled the West's Industrial Revolution was still there for the taking, underlay the subprime mortgage debacle which set off the banking crisis of 2007. Indeed, almost as soon as it was closed in reality the frontier reopened virtually. From 1918 onwards, the empires began to reinterpret themselves as property-owning democracies: the land bank had shut down, but everyone could have a share in the dream or memory of it by acquiring – through a financial transaction now, rather than by just grabbing – his own piece of land with his own home on it. The essentially limited nature of the resource that is land was disguised by making it tradeable – but tradeable in a transaction, a mortgage purchase, which it would take a lifetime to complete, since the so-called asset was essential to life, and the price would necessarily rise to a level represented by an average lifetime's work. What we have recently been seeing in the world's capital markets is a repricing of those shares in the dream or memory of the frontier against shares in the promise of output by the workers in the Eastern regions that are undergoing their own industrial revolutions. Since so much of the market for their products was provided by consumers who paid for them in securitized frontier dreams, they too will face a crisis, the result of which must be an equalization of living standards between the landowning North and the newly industrial, and industrious, South. That equalization will be felt by the landowners as an increase in competition and relative impoverishment – let us hope it is not also felt on one side or the other as an occasion for war.

If that worst of all possible outcomes is to be avoided, America and Europe will have to bury their religious disagreements and recognize that they share a common project.

For the common project does exist. The European Union and the USA are both attempting to fuse together the peoples of old Europe into a political and cultural unit, free from internal violence and dedicated both to democracy and to free trade as the two instruments by which the global economic order can be developed and humanized. However, America and Europe had different experiences of the closure of the nineteenth-century frontier. That difference explains, at least partially, the difference in their reactions to the end of the great divergence in the world order that began with the European Industrial Revolution, and to the prospect of a return to economic parity between the world's regions that is most dramatically represented by the reindustrialization of India and China. America experienced the closure of the frontier, the discovery of the limits to liberty, through a civil war that founded a nation – it experienced, though it never consciously acknowledged, the *constitutive* power of military force. For Europe the end of the frontier, of the era of territorial expansion, that is, of land-grabbing, meant an international war which diminished and impoverished its participants – it experienced the *destructive* power of military force. In the period after 1945, therefore, America and Europe, having learnt in different ways the Hegelian lessons that you can form political units only through constraint and that you cannot live life on the frontier forever, approached in rather different ways

79

the task of relating their common project to the world as a whole.

In America, to which they had emigrated, the project of bringing together the peoples of old Europe was achieved by fusing them – ultimately by unacknowledged force – into a nation (*e pluribus unum*), and in 1918, and again in 1945, America set about reordering the territories of the nineteenth-century empires into self-determining nations like itself. This corresponded, of course, to a genuine aspiration of many of the peoples concerned, but underestimated the practical difficulties of securing agreement between them about which peoples and what land belonged to which nation. American military power came increasingly to be the arbiter of disputes around the world and had to be expanded to a historically unprecedented degree in order to liberate the colonies of the Soviet Empire. Europe, by contrast, had had enough of military force and, under the shield of American protection, sought another way to bring its peoples together: not through making them into one nation, as America so successfully has done, but by persuading their many nations to surrender some of their sovereignty and identity to supranational bodies. This model has been remarkably successful in Europe itself, and in the world at large has been more successful than we may at first realize. The World Trade Organization, with its Dispute Settlement Body, bears more resemblance to a European supranational institution than to any previous treaty-based arrangement for intergovernmental cooperation. But the weakness of the European version of the common project is evident in its origins and has not been remedied with time: it depended from the start on a military guarantee which it could not provide for itself and which was provided instead by America. Time and again in recent years, in the Balkans, in Iraq, in Georgia, the absence of a coherent European defence policy has become all too apparent. There will therefore need to be a fairly radical shift of the perspective in which America and Europe see their mutual relationship. As America shrinks in relative economic significance it will need to learn from Europe the value, and necessity, of accepting the restrictions imposed by supranational and intergovernmental bodies. As military, and especially nuclear, power becomes more dispersed around the world in consequence of economic growth, Europe will need to recover a sense of the value and mission of NATO. Only together can European and American experience provide the basis for a global economic – and so, political – order. Both Europe and America will also have to learn to see the world as once again what it cyclically has been over the last 2,000 years: a structure not of nations but of empires, an agglomeration of nations, nation-like polities, regional hegemonic powers whose military strength provides local stability, and supranational and global authorities whose powers, effectiveness and degree of coordination may be hoped to increase with time.

In 2007, a historical process began which at some point in the near future will culminate in an event which will give its character to the rest of the twenty-first century. One way or the other, that event will be an American decision. In the course of the historical process either the American religion will finally evaporate in the conflict with reality or it will prove so deeply rooted that rather than abandon it America will condemn the world to disorder, violence, poverty and environmental degradation. The collapse of the global credit balloon has revealed the realities that were always there to see: that economic and political structures, the market and the state, cannot exist in isolation from each other. As a market grows, so must the state structure that underwrites and protects it and in the extreme case uses its monopoly of force to maintain the rule of law which enforces private contracts. There is nothing untoward or unexpected about recent massive interventions by governments to protect the international system of credit. A guarantee of this kind is always implicit in the contractual agreements concluded in the markets. The credit collapse is due to a perception that the expansion of the global market over the last 20 years has not been matched by a corresponding visible expansion in the power of the global political institutions to underpin, regulate and enforce market transactions.

The return to regulation now widely demanded could have two totally different outcomes, and the centenary of 1914, which whatever else happens is virtually bound to mark the economic realignment of the world's great regions, could have two totally different aspects. Two years after the American election of 2012 we shall be halfway into what (barring assassinations and palace revolutions) will be either the second term of an avowedly multilateralist president, or the first term of a president elected for his, or her, opposition to all Obama stands for. If at that decisive moment the American religion prevails – the belief that human society can be constructed and maintained purely through private transactions in the markets without the intervention of state power – and if America therefore does not give the necessary political support to the global economic networks it has done so much to bring about, then the prospects are gloomy indeed. If, with recession dragging on and with false dawns and currency crises succeeding one another, America seeks to put the process of interconnection into reverse, to reduce foreign ownership of its assets, and to retreat from the world stage, and from its twentieth-century role of securing global economic interaction, then not only will it fail in its attempt to preserve its privileged living standards, but 2014 will mark the twenty-first century as another century of slump and war. Alternatively, the interconnection already achieved could be an incentive to find a collaborative and peaceful way out of the current crisis. If America can recognize that it not only has to pay its debts but also has to accept the existence of a supranational authority to ensure that it does, if it can recognize the constitutive role of force in political institutions and that its own transcendent military power has to stand behind any authority to which it submits, then there is good hope for the continuance of world order and prosperity. Every major country has an interest in the health of the businesses and the stability of the institutions of its competitors and trading partners. If the reintroduction of regulation means a recognition of the fundamental role of the state power, not just in remedying market failure but also in guaranteeing the existence and security of the market itself, then 2014 could be the moment when the twenty-first century is revealed as an era of global cooperation in which average standards of living will rise considerably, though those who are currently the planetary super-rich will have to content themselves with being poorer than their parents but considerably more honest.

Chapter 6

Saving the World

Saving the banks may not quite amount to saving the world, but it is a first step on the road. For most of us, it has not proved a difficult step and has involved no greater hardship than long hours at the television watching, first, cardboard boxes being removed from offices, and then politicians eating such words as 'efficient markets' and 'light-touch regulation'. But there are some harder steps to come. The consumer boom of the last 20 years was a boom on tick, provided by then friendly banks, and the loans are now being called in, either by the banks themselves or by the governments that have had to nationalize their obligations. All those SUVs and VCRs, all those timeshares in Florida and second homes in Provence, all those dinners in gourmet restaurants and holidays in exotic locations now have to be paid for in longer work and lower salaries, in reduced savings and pensions and restricted opportunities for the young. It will be an unusual experience for citizens of the First World – working to pay off what they (or their parents) owe to the still buoyant Third. Resenting the reversal of fortune, we may be tempted to repudiate our past by inflating away our currency. But beyond such a debauch lies the prospect of a worse hangover still: a flight from the mountain of sovereign debt issued by countries which were once the richest and most reliable debtors in the world but whose word is no longer trusted. The collapse of the global financial system would then have been merely postponed, not averted; and far from avoiding a repetition of the 1930s, we would be condemned to relearn their grimmest lesson: that the consequences of the crash of 1929 were overcome only by the enormous boost to demand and so to production created by general rearmament and the preparations for the Second World War. That lesson is partly moral and partly practical.

Morally, it reminds us that credit, as its name implies, is belief in a promise, that money is a promise to deliver something other than money in the future, and that in a crash people stop fulfilling their own promises and stop believing in the promises of others. They become less willing to entrust the product of their labour to others, since they are less sure that they will get in exchange what they want or need. A collapse in the economy of promises (a credit crunch) is followed by a collapse in the economy of activity (a recession). Credit is restored when people start believing each other again and start once more to have experiences of promises being kept and of real goods and services being exchanged for each other through the medium of money. Over the past 30 years or so, colossal promises were made of future delivery, which are now being withdrawn. No doubt most of those promises were not knowingly fraudulent, but many of them were reckless, and once even those who made cautious promises find themselves unable to fulfil them, thanks to the failure of others, promises themselves fall into disrepute and we lose faith in the future.

If we lose faith in others and in the future, we damage ourselves. We become not only fearful and suspicious but also selfish, miserly and hard. We stop giving to those in need, since charity begins at home, and we see no point in arrangements with strangers – international agreements and institutions, for example – which do not guarantee an immediate advantage to ourselves. If the lifeboat is leaking, the first person to go overboard should be the stranger in our midst – so send the immigrants back home. If we face unemployment here, jobs should not be exported to car factories in Czechoslovakia – protectionism is suddenly politically mentionable, even correct. No one else will look after our interests for us – we had best make sure we can defend ourselves. That was the route to war in the Great Depression, when Germany – in part responding, it must be said, to treatment in kind already meted out to it by the victors of 1918 – withdrew from the League of Nations; began to expel its ancient immigrants, the Jews; and prepared to stand up for itself in a hard Darwinian world in which only the fittest survive. It will be the route to war again, if we do not counter the loss of trust in others and in the institutions by which we cooperate with them, a loss of trust that is all too likely a consequence of rediscovering that ultimately we have no better a guarantor of our money than our local national government.

But the 1930s teach a practical lesson, too. There has to be a real basis in the economy of activity for any revival of confidence in the economy of promises. The Great Depression ended when general preparation for conflict created enough shared understanding about what, for the present at least, needed to be done, and what everyone would do, for the exchange of goods and labour to resume. Similarly, the Long Depression, which began in 1873, ended only with the scramble for Africa in the mid-1880s. International trade, so magnificently and beneficially globalized over the last three decades, cannot recover unless it has better foundations than the globalization of unregulated credit which made the fortunes of bankers. In our present crisis, we have now almost certainly reached the point at which manipulating the machinery of promises alone will not help us. If governments, alone or in collaboration, can come up with nothing better than financial devices – however grandiose – they will simply be repeating the errors of the immediate past. Finance is not enough, for the crisis is no longer simply financial. There must be real new demand, and demand requires other kinds of confidence in the future besides the confidence that money will retain its value and debts will be paid. There must be a confidence that there is a need that can and will be met, and that it will continue – a confidence that is not a passing vogue like that for Dutch tulips, or the title deeds of derelict properties, which merely gives rise to asset bubbles which one day will burst, but a confidence that represents a shared understanding of what is worthwhile, a shared value that is not simply monetary, a shared purpose. These certainties were provided for national populations in the 1930s by the preparation for war in defence of national identities, by confidence in the commitment of governments to attain their military goals and by a shared sense of the value of all fellow citizens engaged in the common project.

Plainly we do not – yet – want to solve our economic problems by having a war. But do we – yet – strongly enough desire the alternative? Wars, when they come, are dramatic and memorable, extreme events arousing extreme passions. The achievement of peace, the avoidance of drama and passion, is little noticed, and the disaster that did not happen is rarely remembered. The Great Event of 1815 was not the Battle of Waterloo

(Napoleon was doomed anyway) but the Congress of Vienna, which gave Europe a stable political structure that lasted a century. It may not be dramatic, but there is an alternative to global depression and international conflict and, immediately after the recent American presidential election, Al Gore pointed it out in the *New York Times*. Few, however, seem to have noticed that he was not simply reiterating his well-known view that something must be done to head off climate change. He was saying – in an article published on 9 November 2008 – that just as the current economic crisis and the current environmental crisis both owe their present severity to the hectic economic activity of the last 30 years, so the solution to the one is the solution to the other. The real new demand, and the confidence in a collective future, which in the 1930s was created for individual nations by the prospect of war among themselves, can in the second decade of the twenty-first century be created by a collective war on climate change and world poverty. We have at the most ten years to prevent a global rise in temperature that will kill billions. The greatest danger in the economic crisis is that it will combine with environmental degradation – that is, more frequent and more severe natural catastrophes – and with indefensible inequalities in the distribution of wealth, to destroy the international system of cooperation developed since 1945. Gore was suggesting that the remedy for worldwide recession is not simply a financial 'rescue package' but the recognition of a physical and continuing need that we all share and that we all need to labour together to meet: the maintenance on our planet of an environment in which the human race can survive. Gore pointed out the obvious economic advantages to the USA, and to any First World government, of using public money not just to rescue banks but also to adapt industry to produce and consume green energy: whether from a revived nuclear sector or from any other carbon-free source. He should, however, have stressed more than he did the economic as well as the environmental case for urgent and drastic collective action. The lesson of the 1930s is that the effects of a once-in-a-lifetime collapse of confidence can be undone only by an epochal change of the first magnitude – such, for example, as a declaration of a group of governments that at a certain point in the not too distant future, no more than five years hence, they will begin to phase out fossil-fuel-driven vehicles (at present responsible for about 20 per cent of global CO_2 emissions) and that state aid similar to that currently being offered to the financial sector will be made available to the motor industry to enable it to adapt. The replacement of the world's stock of automobiles over a deliberately compressed period would be a stimulus to the real economy comparable to a rearmament programme, and of rather more value to everyone on the planet. And even if the planetary conscience of national governments is limited, the geopolitical advantages of such a project should be as evident to the oil-dependent economies of Europe and North America as the internal political advantages to be expected in dealings with organized labour.

Gore, however – mindful perhaps of his audience – did not choose to emphasize that since the environmental challenge is itself by definition global, the political response to it has to be global too. The non-military war can be waged only if the deficiencies of the most recent phase of globalization are repaired: the almost exclusive concentration on the freedom of movement of capital, at the expense of the freedom of movement of labour; the failure to achieve an equitable reduction in barriers to free trade which would take account of the needs of developing industries and economies; and the neglect of the international institutional framework which alone can establish these political preconditions for an economic cooperation not built on sand.

The present crisis is fraught with danger. But for that reason it also offers an extraordinarily exciting opportunity. The collapse of the institutions, and the illusory certainties, that maintained the expansion of world trade after the 1950s offers the chance of a reconstruction that over the next century could underwrite peaceful development, a rebalancing of the world economy and a united response to environmental challenge. What is needed is a mechanism for linking the governmental structures that the world already has – especially the existing national governments – to a world market that is too large for any nation to support or regulate on its own. The mechanism needs to include a certain feedback function so that it becomes more powerful as global economic interrelatedness increases. Such a mechanism was suggested in the 1970s by the late James Tobin.

Tobin, a Nobel laureate in economics, proposed that there should be a worldwide tax on international currency transactions, to be set somewhere between 0.01 and 1 per cent. He saw the tax as a means for discouraging excessive currency speculation and did not at first specify any use to which the revenue it raised should be put. However, it was soon suggested that the considerable sums involved – with the turnover in the currency markets running at $3 trillion a day – could be applied to meeting the United Nations Millennium Development Goals, and perhaps to funding the United Nations Organization itself. None of these purposes, however, appealed sufficiently to the self-interest of governments, and despite the support of economists, and latterly of Gordon Brown, the Tobin tax has remained just a good idea. But maybe it is a good idea whose time has come. For if set at an appropriate level, a Tobin Tax could be used to set up a stabilization fund that could guarantee the world's banking system with resources considerably greater than those readily available to individual central banks. It could even take over the enormous debts those banks are currently incurring and so relieve the public finances of the relevant states. Such a fund, too, would grow faster or more slowly as international activity increased or diminished, and the tax rate could even be calibrated according to the degree of systemic risk the fund managers saw in certain types of transaction or in order to adjust the cost of dealing in over- or undervalued currencies. Since financial stability is now plainly in the interests of everyone, there is a chance that governments will at last band together and agree to a tax that can provide it. Lord Turner, as the chairman of the United Kingdom's Financial Services Authority, indicated in 2009 an interest in global taxes on financial transactions and was roundly condemned by those who would have to pay them. The opposition usually misunderstood, or misrepresented, the Tobin tax as an instrument for a national government to impose order and accountability on its own overmighty banks and argued that by one means or another the banks should simply be made smaller. Both Turner and Tobin, however, were concerned with a world-sized problem, needing a world-sized solution, and in April 2009 the G20 nations made a first attempt to find one.

The first G20 meeting in London agreed to extend considerably the International Monetary Fund's provision for Special Drawing Rights. These have to be financed by the member states. However, if the Fund is to be the

lender of last resort to states that find themselves obliged
to pick up the bill for defaulting global banks, domiciled
in their national jurisdictions, the potential demands on
the IMF's resources have already outgrown the capacity
even of Special Drawing Rights. The IMF needs a revenue
source that comes directly from the global market itself
and so is of a magnitude to stabilize the global market in
case of need. The day may come when the UK or even
the USA would welcome the possibility of selling to the
IMF some of the debt they have incurred in saving their
banks; and only if it had a Tobin tax to draw on could the
IMF save them, and with them the world financial system.
Armed with such a tax, the IMF could become the first
autonomous agent of the political globalization that is
needed to complement and control economic globalization – autonomous because its powers would no longer
be solely dependent on the goodwill of its members. It
would be natural for the Fund to take over from national
governments the task of regulating the transnational
banking from which it would draw its income. But it
would also be natural for a lender with such resources to
become, through its Special Drawing Rights, the effective
manager of a global reserve currency, which, as the Bank
of China pointed out recently, was originally a part of the
world economic settlement that Keynes envisaged in 1945.
(However, the Bank of China did not note that it was also
part of Keynes's scheme that governments should be fined

for persistently running excessive surpluses on their trade balances.) A global tax – and a Tobin tax could only be imposed globally – is moreover the only plausible way of paying for global public goods. The IMF could – perhaps through the World Bank – deploy its Tobin resources for the attainment of the Millennium Goals. Indeed, without some such support the Goals are likely to be obliterated entirely by the present crisis. Yet in the long run, gross inequalities of wealth and opportunity are as much a threat to global stability as the excesses of bankers. So too, of course, is the impending climatic catastrophe: set at the higher level of 1 per cent, the tax could easily raise the $2 trillion a year that Lord Stern reckons is necessary to reduce carbon emissions to a manageable level. Similarly, the reform of the United Nations, essential if that organization is to play a part in the future political management of the global market, is unlikely to happen unless its budget is made both independent of national contributions and subject to effective scrutiny by another international agency – as it could be if the IMF became its paymaster.

Global monetary policy could be the instrument that makes global governance possible. If the Great Event proves to be the conversion of the USA to that goal, then the establishment of a Tobin tax could be the practical step that not merely saves the world's banks but also inaugurates a century of peace, growth and environmental prudence. The goal is not utopian – global governance is not synonymous with a world-state. Once we have freed ourselves from the illusion that the only actors on the world stage are nation-states, we can see that there is already such a thing as global civil society, and according to Hegel it is at the level of civil society that the first forms of public governance are born (called by him 'corpora-tions' or, in a special sense, 'police'). Global civil society is the already existing precursor of the global political order, of which a reformed IMF could be the first supranational instrument.

Global civil society, however, is not peopled only by bank-ers. It is an aspect of all of us; it is all those international aspects of our lives which are institutionalized but not part of the governmental or intergovernmental structure. Its weightiest single component, the non-governmental institution which gives most concrete expression to our international existence, is the multinational corporation. To be an employee or shareholder or customer of BP or Coca-Cola is not to be disloyal to your local state or your compatriots: it is to exist already at the global level at which peace and prosperity can be secured for the future. A multinational that fosters its own company-wide code of conduct is already contributing to the formation of a global ethic. Another, and much older, institution of global civil society is the republic of letters, the net-work of academies, learned societies and links between scholars, journalists, writers and artists, which even more consciously has for centuries been building up a common image of humanity. A third element, of course, are NGOs, which evidently have a role in global civil society, like other voluntary associations, but it is important to realize their limitations. They require no apology when they represent a particular interest group, such as trades unionists or the disabled or regional producers of particular commodities (sugar, for example). But when they exist only to voice concerns about a range of issues that are not germane to the economic well-being of their members, they face a certain problem of legitimacy. Unlike the governments whose actions they seek to influence, they are not the chosen representatives of the people for whom and to whom they are responsible. Indeed, they are usually not responsible to anyone: if their advice proves disastrously wrong, it is not they who will be voted out of office. They are responsible, in other words, not to the people whose interests they speak for but to their image of those people – they are responsible to their conscience, and conscience is the force that drives them. Such a problem does not arise for the churches, international NGOs that do not have to apologize for being the voice of conscience: that is what they are understood to be, and if they are heard, that is how they are heard.

Whatever the institutions through which it speaks, the voice of the human conscience is the voice that most needs to be heard as we approach the Great Event. It should be articulating above all the value of the common good, the good of all humanity in so far as that good can be achieved by political action, by global governance. That means speaking for the development of political institutions that can act for the common good, that can create checks and balances to counter the use of political power – that is, in the end, the power of violence – on behalf of sectional interests. It does not mean calling for the development of political institutions that are themselves motivated by conscience – that is a call either for an absurdity or for a theocracy, in so far as the two are distinct. And it does not mean calling for the political direction of economic behaviour – that too is either an absurdity or fascism, in so far as the two are distinct. In fact, it means virtually the opposite: calling, and working, for an end to the political manipulation of economic life to the benefit of the rich at the expense of the poor, for the true liberalization of world trade, for the elimination of all barriers that make labour less mobile than capital, for the establishment and financing of lasting political institutions with a global reach, and so for a globalization that is worthy of the name.

Part II

Finding the Way

Chapter 7

Three Principles of Political Economy

We don't hear much about political economy these days. Despite the importance to J. M. Keynes of Cambridge's Political Economy Club, the words now have a musty, defunct aura, suggesting Victorian reading rooms, titles like 'Gradgrind on Rent' and dismal, secular sermons. They also suggest something obsoletely amateurish, lacking rigorous definitions and methods. Whatever it was, political economy is generally assumed to have been replaced in the modern world by science, or by several sciences: politics, sociology, economics, all of them, but especially the last, boasting their quantitative method and their mathematical basis. By the study of 'rational choice', 'game theory' and 'efficient markets', the fields unsystematically traversed by Smith and Mill, Sidgwick and Marshall are thought to have been given a distinctness and certainty comparable to that of the predictive natural sciences. Except, of course, that the new disciplines failed to predict the arrival of the greatest economic disaster for 80 years, even in August 2007 when it was coming through the door. Anatole Kaletsky[*] has laid much of the blame for the disaster itself on the academic illusion that economics could be an exact science, even though it is perfectly obvious that it cannot (if it could, everyone who learned it could become the richest person in the world). The illusion that mathematical modelling could set the gambling machines permanently to 'jackpot' was as welcome to politicians in pursuit of votes as it was to bankers in pursuit of bonuses. After the return to reality, Kaletsky believes, economics, if it is to survive, must abandon the attempt to predict the unpredictable and 'must broaden its horizons to recognize the insights of other social sciences and historical studies . . . [The insights of] Smith, Keynes, Hayek, Schumpeter and the other truly great economists . . . came from historical knowledge, psychological intuition and political understanding. Their analytical tools were words not mathematics'. To put it another way, economics will have to return to its origins, to the study of political economy.

The separation of economics from politics over the last century or so has been as damaging, both in practice

---

[*] Anatole Kaletsky, 'Goodbye, homo economicus', *Prospect*, 26th April 2009.

and in theory, as the siren song of mathematics. Practical political argument, as well as argument in the academy, assumed that markets and governments had quite different spheres of competence, and focused on the desirability of governments 'intervening' when markets 'failed'. The concept of 'market failure', however, begged the most important question of all, for it concealed that markets rely on governments not just to rescue them when they go wrong but also to exist in the first place. Without a state power to guarantee the security of property, to enforce contracts through its courts and to protect the integrity of the medium of exchange by its maintenance of a stable currency and its supervision of the money supply, markets cannot be set up and cannot last. If you cannot be confident you will not be robbed on your way to and from the marketplace, if you have to be a relative of the storeholder before you can trust him to keep his word, if you cannot be sure that the money you receive at the counter where you sell will be honoured at the counter where you buy, the market town is unlikely to develop into a trade centre. In the early 1990s, Russia failed to make the transition to a market economy as much for political as for economic reasons: it failed to establish a trustworthy state. Governments do not 'intervene' – they are there all the time: and markets are successful because the towns, the polities, where they are held are well run – well 'policed', as it used to be said.

If economics and politics can be brought back together again, as they will have to be if the current crisis is to be understood and mastered, and a future worse calamity is to be avoided, the reconstituted discipline of political economy will need clarity about three basic principles.

I.   First, there needs to be clarity about some differences. **The first principle of political economy is that the state, the market and society are different beasts, and that political economy is the study of the relation between the state and the market.** Politics, economics and sociology have been able to drift apart because there are three different forces that determine human social interaction. There is the fear – that is, the threat – of death, which human beings in combination can impose upon each other in that political association which, in its developed form, is called the state. There is, secondly, the need for what maintains life – for food and other sources of heat – which, again in combination, human beings satisfy in their economic relations. And, thirdly, there is the desire for reproduction (of which the desire for sexual congress is only one subjective and individual aspect), which, through affective and interpersonal relationships, constructs the systems of mutual care and support that we call society, and that guarantee us a collective future.

It has long been recognized that the state, with its command of the instruments of force, is thereby distinguished from the market, where the needs of all parties are accommodated to each other (always, of course, with some element of compromise) through an exchange of the products of labour which is, and has to be, free. Franz Oppenheimer (1864–1943) therefore saw the state as an improper means of bringing force to bear on economic transactions and so as institutionalized robbery, and he passed on this view of the state to the libertarian American economists who were his pupils. Oppenheimer, however, made the mistake of assuming that the state made use of force merely as a short cut to acquiring the goods traded in the market. Max Weber saw more deeply into the matter and recognized that the state, as the monopoly owner of the power of force in a given territory, had a role of its own, and that the realm in which the proper application of force was decided was the realm of politics. Through political mechanisms we decide what laws shall constrain other members of our state, even though we shall never be physically present to impose them. The law does not bind us through an economic transaction, for it is the law that guarantees the integrity of economic transactions in the first place (by defining and preventing fraud, for example). The law binds us through the sanction of physical force. If we do not do as the sovereign (political power) decrees, we shall eventually be subject to physical constraint – thrown into prison or put to death, or, if our resistance is collective, subjugated by the army. On that threat reposes not just the possibility of state tyranny, as the libertarians fear, but also the power of the state to define and defend our liberties, to prevent the infringement of what it defines as our rights and to maintain the peace, order and trust which are the prerequisites for the functioning of the market. The market for its part depends on the absence from its operations of the threat of force. If a man fingers a knife while suggesting that I sell to him rather than to another, the market cannot establish a price for what I am selling. Equally, there cannot be a market price established between a supplier of the necessities of life and a buyer in immediate need of them. What price will a starving family pay for bread? A transaction under the threat of death is not exchange but enslavement. By keeping the ultimate and infinite threat of death out of the marketplace, by suppressing rackets and by imposing minimal conditions for the survival of its members (by distributing bread in time of famine, for example), the state ensures that *only* the relative needs of all parties – not the intimidation of one party by the threat of violence – determine the exchange of goods and labour and the (finite) price at which the exchange occurs. Moreover, by guaranteeing security of tenure against robbers or enemies who would take it violently away, the state enables those it has defined as owners to let their property out for rent. The result is a structure in which all the manifold needs and desires of our personal lives, in so far as they can be satisfied by labour and its products, are brought into relationship with the similar needs and desires of others – of very many others, most of whom are and will always remain unknown to us and may be subject to the jurisdiction of different states. Relationships here are far more complex than mere relationships of power. I cannot satisfy all my wants, but through the market I can satisfy a reasonable proportion of them by satisfying the wants of others. By being given a price, the work I do can not only be exchanged for the goods that feed me but also, through the bank with which my greengrocer saves, be used by a property developer in Singapore to pay his builders' wages. The breadth, depth and subtlety of the market is vastly greater than that of any system of law and political control, and most of it is unknown and unknowable by an individual, much as the unconscious is unknowable by the conscious mind. But just as we rely on the simplifications of our conscious mind to guide the unknown complexities of our bodies though the physical world, so we need the simplicity of the state, founded on the ultimately simple sanction of force, to guide the operations of the market.

There is of course a third area of our collective life which is subject neither to the simple exigency of force that defines the political realm nor to the practice of priced exchange in the economy. The desire of couples for reproduction first manifests itself to others in the founding of families, which with their extended kinship structures are the basis of what we call society. As members of an essentially social species, we human beings seek to reproduce not just our bodies but also the relationships with other personalities through which our own personalities have been formed: we have known parents as providers and authorities, and also as the sick and dependent; we have known children and teachers, and friends towards whom our feelings are coloured by emotions first learned in the family; in certain traditions we have a powerful sense of what it means to be an uncle, a grandmother, a nephew, a cousin, a godparent. 'Society' is these relationships understood as binding the human race together through all the variations of the erotic drive: heterosexual and homosexual, parental and infantile, loving and aggressive, sublimated, moral and altruistic. Hospitals and schools, the institutional care of the orphaned and the elderly, associations of the charitable and the likeminded, sports and social clubs all grow out of the feeling that we are or should be one family, caring collectively for those we have engendered or who engendered us. When that family feeling encounters its limits, when we come up against others who, we think, do not belong, or who do not wish to belong, tribalism and nationalism are born – physical violence against those who are not part of our reproductive group.

However, because our concept of 'society' reposes

on the fiction that we can all be bodily present to one another, as in an extended family, sociology, as the study of 'society', cannot be a part of political economy. For the family is not an adequate image of the complexity of human relationships, rooted though it is in the original sociability of our species. Its power is abruptly ended if tribalism leads to feuding and the state steps in to restore order – to assert, in other words, the interests of those beyond the family, however extended. But even if the limits of the family are not defined by the political exercise of force, they reveal themselves as its members try to make a living. The family cannot accommodate extensive relationships with those whom we do not know. It is an image of a world in which everyone knows everyone else and, as on an internet social site, all relationships are personal. But, as Hegel said in his *Philosophy of Right*, there comes a time when we have to grow up and leave the family and go out into a world of work for people we do not know and will never meet, the world of the market. 'Society' has to give way to the economy.

Certainly, our collective life is not exhausted by the economic relations established in the market, the 'system of needs and their satisfactions', as Hegel calls it, nor by the power relations that are imposed by the state, but it is not exhausted by what we think of as 'society', either. All three ways of imagining collective existence are ways of imagining the interaction of physical human bodies – as the objects of force, as the locus of needs and their satisfactions, as agents of the reproduction of distinctively human life. But there is a fundamental difference between the state and the market on the one hand and society on the other. The state and the market are collections of human beings in which, in fact and in principle, dealings are between parties who are not physically acquainted. They are the means by which the human species has learned to establish structured relationships between very large numbers of people who do not know each other personally, and never can. Dealing with this ignorance (through such deliberately impersonal concepts as the impartiality of justice or the fair market price) is the essential feature that marks them off from 'society'. 'Society', by contrast, is a collectivity whose members – whatever the facts of the matter – are imagined as knowing, or at least as capable of knowing, each other physically and personally. Political economy is the study of the interrelation between the two forms of collective life in which human beings are physically and personally unknown to each other.

II. **The second principle of political economy, therefore, has to be that, distinct though they are, the state and the market, as collectivities in which the majority of the members are not known to each other, are nonetheless linked – intrinsically, by money, by tax, by the vote and, in recent history, by the public sphere.** From the earliest stages of civilization, the public institution of money has brought the state and the market together and related us politically and economically to those we do not know. (While within the family or society money has always been thought of as tainting relations, as betraying or prostituting them, bringing them into a political or economic arena where they do not belong.) Money has its function from the market, and its value – its validity – from the state. Caesar stamps his image on the coin, and as long as the labourer and the shopkeeper know that Caesar has control of his armies, the coin will be accepted by the one as a wage for his work (instead of goods) and by the other as payment for his goods (instead of work). Why? Because he who controls the system of force also controls the system of law. By assuring all parties that he will enforce the terms of a contract, even if the desires of the parties alter with time, Caesar makes it possible to trade promises through an impersonal and enduring medium of exchange – a currency. His coin passes through many hands before and after it comes into mine. As it does so, it exchanges one promise for another, and Caesar's image is the guarantee that those promises will be carried out. When bankers, having pledged the same coins many times, fail to honour their accumulated promises, Caesar has to maintain his own credit, not just by crucifying the bankers (though the populace enjoys the spectacle) but also by persuading others to meet the bankrupts' obligations – for example, by striking new coins in a round of quantitative easing.

But the coin of the trader is also the coin of the tribute. By its monopoly over the threat of death, the state not only maintains a system of law which permits a market to exist but also acquires its most significant power to intervene in the market: the power to tax. Taxes are not payments made in the course of an exchange transaction (I am not paying the city rates officer to empty my dustbin as I might pay a private contractor): taxes are payments made under sanction of law, that is, under the threat of force. They may be imposed – whether as disincentives or as revenue raisers – for any collective purpose: political (such as the maintenance of the armed forces or of the administrators of the law), economic (such as the provision of trans-port and communications or other infrastructure which develops the market or makes it more efficient) or social (such as furthering cohesion and continuity by caring for the sick or by educating the next generation). Tax is one of the means by which my activity in the market becomes an activity of the state that makes the market possible. (Which is why it is absurd to say that there is a date in the tax year before which I am working for the government and only after which I am working 'for myself'.) It is a characteristic of the modern state and the modern market that their memberships increasingly overlap: that all are taxed (not just the peasants as in the pre-revolutionary world) and that all benefit from tax revenues (not just the monarch, the bureaucracy or the poor). By the same token it is characteristic of modernity that the state power itself is universally distributed (rather than reserved to particular classes or families). In a democratic state – in what Kant calls a republic – all those who are subject to the law have a hand in making it. By means of the vote, we all share in deciding how the monopoly power of force shall be applied to ourselves collectively: what taxes the law shall impose and how it shall decree that the market shall be assisted, underwritten or regulated.

The colossal disproportion between the scale of modern political or economic activity and the individual agents who take part in it, the apparent impossibility of discerning the relationship between my own decisions and the myriads of other people's decisions that make up the whole system, should not lead us to underestimate the importance of the link between the state and the market that is established by the vote. Ultimately, it is on the power of the vote that the operation of another distinctively modern intermediary between the state and the market depends, what Habermas has taught us to call the public sphere. The public sphere, in the sense used here (which is not exactly Habermas's usage), is a means of making conscious and visible to us our economic and political relationships with those who are not known to us personally. It represents the state and the market to us as if they were a society. Its most tangible form is the realm of mass communication – books, newspapers, broadcasting, the internet. These media create an imaginary society in which the means through which we have personal knowledge of each other – language, sight and hearing – are used to give us information about those remote from us in space, or in the chain of economic cause and effect. Perspective is foreshortened so that the millions about whom, or to whom, the information is made available are shrunk to the size of an audience in a studio or a lecture theatre, just as all the multifarious activities of the human race over 24 hours are shrunk to a few inches of headline. And reactions to the information thus condensed become part of the information, too, and are passed on as 'public opinion' (as a collective threat to use the power of the vote) to those who take decisions about the deployment of political power, of the power of force. We may know no one in China, and may consume only a jar or two of cockles in the course of a year, and may never have been to Morecambe Bay, but we learn in our millions through the media of the cruelty and negligence of those who employ Chinese cockle pickers and who callously let them drown, and we want legal and administrative action to be taken against them. When it is, we feel – no doubt rightly – that we live in a humane (that is, *socially* responsible) state, even though the only change in our personal lives is a scarcely perceptible rise in the price of cockles. Through the imaginary society of the public sphere the state has interacted with the market, and some lives, we may hope, have been changed for the better, even though they remain quite unknown to us.

The fundamental problem in modern political economy is not the problem of scale, of the relation of the individual to an ever-vaster collective. The problem is, rather, a mismatch on the largest scale of all: between a market that transcends the jurisdictional boundaries of states, and the market-regulating power of the vote, which can be exercised only within state boundaries. The economic implications of our actions have become global: the fate of families in China is affected by which jar we take down from the supermarket shelf, and conversely the fate of toy manufacturers in Britain is determined by the willingness of Chinese families to live apart for the sake of low wages in distant factories, while the bankers who trade promises shuffle the savings of these same Chinese workers with the house-owning ambitions of subprime borrowers in Louisiana. The media in their foreshortened way may make us aware of some of these connections. But there is no state power with a global reach that can encompass them all in a single system of law, no Caesar who can strike a global currency, nor can we even be certain that any existing state can guarantee enough of the obligations incurred by now retired bankers for their pensions – or anyone else's – to be worth anything in the future. Keynes recognized, of course, that persistent imbalances between surplus and deficit countries would have to be remedied by political action. But the only political instrument available in his time was an international treaty which none have ever been willing to sign. The global economic crisis is, as it was then, necessarily also a crisis of global governance.

III.   What is true of the world order or disorder is true of those caught up in it. **The third principle a revived political economy must adopt is that its starting point cannot be the behaviour of individuals as somehow prior to their political and economic interaction.** There is not and cannot be any such thing as an individual unexposed to the threat of force and unengaged in production and exchange. Politics and economics both suffer if they are separated from each other or from our understanding of human identity. If the market is thought of as a place where pre-existing individuals make rational choices about their own interests, free from external 'intervention', government will be thought of as an irrational constraint on choice, as parasitic on the market and as the enemy of freedom. But there is a market for individual economic agents to act in only because a state guarantees the tenure of property, secures freedom by the rule of law, maintains choice, by the regulation of monopolies, and gives civic identity to individuals by affirming their rights. Hegel properly argued against Rousseau that human beings are born neither free nor equal but are made so by the state of which they are citizens. The deepest implication of his political thinking is that individuality is a social category, in the sense that it is a category of *collective* human life: What it means for us to be individuals is determined by the society that gives us names and a language in which to say 'I' (and in many cases the various due gradations of 'you', 'we' and 'they'), by the economy in which we gradually construct ourselves through our productive work for each other, and by the state that safeguards our physical integrity, prohibits our being sold as chattels, protects our lives and limbs and maintains the institutions within which we can have duties and expectations and freedoms. The freedom to be a shaman or the duty to respect one's totem are as unavailable to members of industrial mass-society as are the right to vote or the freedom of the press or the freedom to pursue the ambition of being a banker or a snooker player to members of a tribe of desert nomads. The individual the consequences of whose choices are investigated by economics is already a social and political being, and the good – that is, just and effective – government whose nature is studied by the political scientist is not simply the government that interferes minimally in economic processes.

Because individuality is a social category, any attempt to describe political or economic life that starts from the assumption, or fiction, that social relationships are something that individuals choose (or once upon a time chose) to enter into, out of a calculation of their own advantage, must fail, and – as the example of the American Bill of Rights shows – must lead to perverse consequences. If individuals are social constructs, the idea that they might have banded together to found, on certain conditions, the society that has constructed them – the idea of a Social Contract – is an absurdity: Baron Münchhausen pulling himself up by his own bootlaces. There is for human beings no such thing as a state of nature out of which they emerged into society. John Rawls, probably the most influential thinker of the late twentieth century, gave new life to the theory of a social contract by stressing its purely hypothetical, rather than historical, status and by adding to it the assumption of what he called 'the veil of ignorance': in order to determine what constituted a just society we were to ask ourselves 'how would the original parties to the social contract have constituted the society they were setting up if they did not know what place they personally would occupy in it once it came into existence?' As a device for focusing our minds on what in practice we regard as a 'fair' arrangement, as 'impartial', or 'impersonal' justice, the veil of ignorance is brilliantly effective. But it cannot found a theory of social relations in general. Plainly, the contracting parties cannot choose not to belong to a reproductive group – not to have parents or other relatives – nor can they choose to be exempt from the obligation to fix a price if they wish to exchange commodities with another group, and they certainly cannot exempt themselves from the threat of violence from others whom they can control only by opposing to them a similar threat. In all these respects individuals ineluctably already know themselves to be part of a network, a collectivity – to be both reproducers and reproduced, buyers and sellers, agents and patients of violence – before they start to reflect on how they might adjust or link these relationships. There are some facts about yourself of which you cannot pretend to be ignorant. The scope of Rawls's *A Theory of Justice* is at once too broad and too narrow. On the one hand, it is too broad, because by 'society' Rawls means something that combines all three of the major forms of collective existence that I have distinguished as 'society', the 'market' and the 'state'. Conscious choice and deliberate control – the planned exercise of force to maintain particular structures and procedures – is possible only within the state, and the state is the proper realm of justice. There cannot be, as Rawls wants there to be, a 'just economy'. But there can certainly be just (and unjust) state regulation of economic affairs.* On the other hand, Rawls's concept of a society is too narrow,

---

* While a 'just' or 'fair' price is a price determined solely by the market, uninfluenced by force or favour or by political or personal considerations.

for he explicitly treats it as something 'closed', something cut off from other 'societies'. But there is no such thing as a state-cum-economy-cum-reproductive group that is cut off from the rest of the human race: commercial, political and personal interaction pass across all borders. Or rather there is such a thing, or at least such an idea: there is the idea of the nation in the American ideology. That is what Rawls really means by 'a society'. And that ideology is quite inadequate to the reality of global interdependence. Whatever justice is, it has to be found and established across the planet: it cannot be set up in one country while the rest of the world ripens towards it. If it exists, it exists internationally, in the global agreements that permit or forbid discriminatory trade practices, that prosecute crimes against humanity, that give rights to refugees and economic migrants. Justice cannot be just another edition of American exceptionalism – not even of its humane, Rawlsian version.

To say that the individual components of social systems are themselves social constructs is not to say that individuals do not exist. On the contrary, what is truly individual about our lives cannot be an object of the social sciences of politics, economics and sociology: the threat of death is constitutive of politics, but my death is of no political significance in itself and is merely the limit to my political existence; our need for things to consume drives the economic system, but the moment of consumption lies outside that system altogether and terminates the process of exchange; society is founded on our desire to reproduce ourselves, but the sexual act, the shared satisfaction of desire which begins and ends the social process, is not a social act. No one else can die for me, eat for me or love for me. Nor can anyone else do my duty for me. As an individual, I relate to other individuals through an ethical imperative, the imperative to do good in my situation of limited knowledge, limited life and limited influence. That ethical imperative founds my moral life and enables me to understand myself as a unique embodied spirit, as the purpose for which the economic and political systems exist, as a named, individual, receiver and transmitter of life. But the imperative itself is not an object of political, economic or social science. Rawls's theory attempts to subject political, economic and social life to the individual's ethical obligation to do good. But as soon as we think of ourselves as political, economic or social agents, we become something that can be understood only through the systems of which we are then components – systems which do not die, in which the circle of production and consumption is endless and of which the potential scope is planetary. The ideal relation between the state and the market can be determined only by political bodies that operate at the global level, the level to which economic activity naturally rises. Rawls, however, thinks it can be determined by imposing an ethical obligation on individuals to criticize their national institutions in the name of justice. That obligation is in turn reduced by him to the rational reflection of supposedly pre-social individuals on what is to their own advantage. The moral obligation, in this analysis, loses its imperative quality – it becomes a calculus of self-interest, as if individuals determined what was good by pricing the consequences of their decisions in a market. Rawlsian, priced, justice is extraordinarily unlike real, moral, justice. Similarly, Rawlsian rational individuals are extraordinarily unlike real individuals, and the isolated and isolationist society they are assumed to found is extraordinarily unlike global economic and political reality. They live behind a hypothetical veil of ignorance about what serves their personal interest but do not share in the huge and uneliminable ignorance that all real individuals have: our ignorance about the consequences for other individuals of our political and economic choices.

It is a characteristic, and perhaps intrinsic, weakness of theories of the Social Contract to demand of ethics what can be provided only by institutions. In the nineteenth and twentieth centuries, the potential scope of the political, economic and social systems began to be actualized and their reach became global. Only a version of political economy that can detach itself from the fiction of pre-social individuality and can rise to rethinking the relation of state and market in terms of global institutions will be adequate to the demands of the twenty-first century and of the Great Event that will inaugurate it.

Chapter 8

Global Institutions or a Global Ethic? What's Wrong with Rights

In 1993, looking towards a future world of poverty, violence, crime and the possible collapse of the ecosystem, the theologian Hans Küng warned, in a draft declaration for the Parliament of the World's Religions: 'there will be no better global order without a global ethic'. He has subsequently devoted much of his time and thought to developing a statement of such an ethic. Maybe he is right: maybe, as he has also famously said, there can be 'no peace among the nations without peace among the religions', and maybe peace among the religions will necessarily involve the conscious formulation of common and fundamental ethical principles. But the relation between ethical principles and ethical life is not straightforward.

Sigmund Freud, for example, had a low opinion of

ethics. In *Civilization and Its Discontents* he defined ethics as 'the attempt by means of a command of the super-ego to attain what all other civilizing activity has hitherto not been able to attain . . . In my view, as long as virtue is not rewarded here on earth, ethics will preach in vain.' Indeed, while rejecting socialist idealism, he went on to say that 'it seems indubitable to me that a material change in people's relations to possessions will bring more relief here than any ethical command'. Yet at the same time he recognized that ethics addresses what he calls 'the sorest point in any civilization', the need to control human aggression. Ethics is crucially important, but its importance is not what its official guardians think. For, as the voice of the super-ego, ethics is the vehicle of humanity's aggression against itself. In telling us to avoid aggression, it subjects us to aggression. The command to love one's neighbour as oneself is not only obviously unnatural and unfulfillable, but by being a command it launches us into a vicious circle; the more we obey it by being unaggressive to others the more we disobey it by being aggressive to ourselves. The punishment for disobedience to the commands of the super-ego is guilt. As if this were not bad enough, Freud in the same essay identifies the process of civilization as a process of the ever-greater extension of the realm of love, 'of Eros, which is seeking to draw together isolated individuals, later families, then tribes, peoples, nations into one great unity, humanity'. The extension of the realm of love, which requires the suppression of aggression, can be achieved only at the cost of the extension of the realm of aggression against those outside the realm. That may mean those who do not heed the commandment to love: 'After the apostle Paul had made the universal love of humanity into the foundation of his Christian community, Christianity's extreme intolerance of those who remained outside was the inevitable consequence.' Or it may mean ourselves, in so far as we allow the command to become the instrument of our internal discipline. The growth of love means the growth of guilt. 'If civilization is the inevitable process of development from the family to humanity, it is indissolubly bound up, . . . as a consequence of the eternal strife between love and the desire for death, with an intensification of the sense of guilt, perhaps to levels which the individual will find intolerable.'

Freud's picture of the human race as caught in a self-reinforcing spiral of ever more complex and intense interaction involving an ever-higher proportion of its members, and as a result in an ever-greater potential for aggression and so in ever-greater guilt, has lost none of its relevance since he first sketched it in 1930. The awareness that we belong to one world is much wider and much deeper than it was 80 years ago, and the economic and political links that bind us to nearly all other human beings are that much clearer. Yet the communications media, in particular television, which Freud knew hardly or not at all, and which can put us into a direct emotional relation with people on the other side of the world, especially those who seem to ask for our love, such as the suffering and destitute, have also made that relationship an occasion of guilt and so of covert or overt aggression. There is so much to feel guilty about nowadays: being white or male or unmotherly or fat, driving a car or using plastic bags – all are sins against love. And the smug ones who can tick all the boxes exude as much passive – or, in the case of the animal rights lobby, active – aggression as the rest of us together manage to channel into our bad consciences. The overt and angry rejection of love by the redneck reactionary is plainly delusive in its denial of the interconnectedness of the world out of which the redneck makes his money, but his aggression is no different in quality from that of his political opponent and is a response to the same reality.

The mutual and progressive reinforcement of Eros and aggression in the production of an ethic of guilt is particularly apparent in the field of sexuality. In 1930, Freud complained that 'Contemporary civilization clearly indicates that it will permit sexual relations only on the basis of the unique and indissoluble binding of one man to one woman, that it dislikes sexuality as an autonomous source of pleasure and is inclined to tolerate it only as a means to the reproduction of human beings for which no replacement has so far been found.' Although that is a view of sex which is probably still held in theory, if not in practice, by a majority of the human race, it would in the English-speaking world be difficult to find many to commit themselves to it publicly other than a certain number of Baptists and Roman Catholic bishops. Yet what has taken its place since Freud wrote is a strange ambivalence, or bifurcation, of attitudes which surely bears out his general analysis. On the one hand, in the realm of what we might call the public imaginary, anything goes: fantasies of non-exclusive, non-reproductive and non-inhibited sexual pleasure are sufficiently acceptable to the mass market to be used to sell everything from perfume to automobiles; and in film, TV and the internet the availability of fictional or real pornography, from soft to hard, from *Friends* via *Big Brother* to blogs of the Mile-High Club, maintains the image of a normality that is at the least polymorphously perverse. (A British newspaper has a regular column, written by a woman, called 'Sleeping Around'.) On the other hand, the same public space is inhabited by a number of sex-related commands which had little or no prominence in Freud's time – against discrimination or stereotyping based on gender or sexual orientation, against non-consensual or under-age sex – which are loaded with a degree of opprobrium which is remarkable given the countervailing attitude of 'anything goes': sex has not ceased to be an area of concern to the super-ego; it's just that the super-ego's concerns seem to have become rather different. The possibility, indeed the certainty, of guilt remains, and given the much greater public visibility of sex, guilt is that much greater, too. Even in 1930, there were still numerous institutional and behavioural safeguards against sexual violence towards women: less prominence in the workplace, less going out unaccompanied, more modesty, as it was called, in dress and language, more fiction of social precedence than we find now. Now, these external precautions have ceased to be available and therefore have to be internalized in the form of commands from the super-ego. Moreover, since the public imaginary requires sexually suggestive dress and behaviour of both women and men, the internal opposition to the commands is that much greater and the commands themselves are that much more severe. Guilt grows, and so does guilt's consequence, depression.

It might at first sight seem, therefore, that the ethical consensus in sexual matters that Freud deplored in 1930 has lost its consensual character and is now in competition with at least two rival attitudes: a politically correct, puritanical, liberationism, and a politically unreflective, if not actually incorrect, hedonism. In fact, however, the strength of Freud's method is that it enables us to see these different changes as parts of a single process: the ever more complex integration of the human race accompanied necessarily by the ever-stricter self-discipline of the individuals who compose it. We are not seeing a break-down of a consensual morality so much as a simultaneous eroticization and moralization of life, an extension both of Eros and necessarily at the same time of aggression, in the form of ethical commands, over all our experience, as a consequence of the successful integration of more and more of the human race into a complex unity. Twenty-four-hour television news links us all across the planet, but no story appears without the implicit or explicit questions attached: what is the moral? what is the issue here that we are obliged to deal with? who is to blame? The weakness of Freud's method, however, is that, because it assumes that the processes it describes begin in the human psyche, it can give only the sketchiest account of the relation of the internal, psychic consequences – the guilt and depression – to an external and material cause. If we want to know what is going on in the real world to bring about the psychopathology that Freud describes we must turn to another thinker who also had a low opinion of ethics, to Hegel.

Hegel notoriously criticized Kant's fundamental principle of morality, the categorical imperative, as an empty abstraction, a mere 'ought', *Sollen*. Ethics, for Hegel, were always embodied in some kind of institution, some stage of social life, of which the individual with his or her conscience was only one. The supreme form of ethical life, that which controls and situates all others, is for Hegel political life, life in the various forms of state. That the state possesses this ultimate ethical role in relation to its citizens is shown in the same moment in which it demonstrates, and tests, its own ethical and political individuality in relation to other states, the moment of war. For war both reduces the significance of the individual, his life and possessions, to nothing, and is the ultimate form of ethical life acknowledged by world history, where in the deepest sense might is right. What Hegel says about the state, and about war, certainly bears the marks of his time and has to be significantly modified in the light of changes in the world's political structure since then, but for our purposes today his understanding of the hierarchy of the forms of ethical life could not be more relevant. The ways in which we understand our selves and our social roles in terms of a series of overlapping obligations, practices and identities – individual, family, economic, civic, political – culminate in an authority which is uniquely defined by its wielding the power of violence, what we may even nowadays continue to call the state. To that extent Hegel is at one with Machiavelli and Hobbes, but also with Weber.

But Hegel can also shed a new light on what we have learned from Freud. Freud had great difficulty convincing his disciples of his discovery, late in life, of two conflicting drives in the human psyche, to love and death, the forces of pleasure and of aggression, Eros and Thanatos. He might have found his task easier if, instead of looking inwards, into the mind, he had looked outwards, into the social world, and allowed himself to be guided by Hegel. There he would have found the origin of the dichotomy in our emotional life which he had identified, but which he could not account for. For desire and aggression are not in the first instance affective drives within individuals but social relations between individuals and groups. Freud is quite right to say that the process of civilization involves the construction of ever more complexly integrated human relations, but he is wrong to attribute that process to the operation of a drive within the human individual to which he gives the name of Eros. That process is far more adequately described by Hegel in his account of the 'system of needs and their satisfactions', which largely corresponds to what we now think of as the economy. Similarly, Freud is quite right to say that the process of civilization also involves a continuous interaction of the integrating power of desire with the ordering and regulating power of force, but he is wrong to describe that contrary power as an internal drive to aggression. Physical force is first of all deployed in the external and physical world, and Hegel and Weber are surely right to identify the external power that uses force to regulate civil society and the economy as the state.

How, then, are we to interpret in Hegel's terms the ever more intimate symbiosis of desire and aggression, Eros and guilt, that Freud has so accurately diagnosed as characteristic of our modern situation? As a first step, we need to consider the most important modification that the last nearly 200 years have made to the picture of political life that Hegel painted around 1820. The crucial change that those two centuries have seen is one that was already apparent to Freud and is the starting point of his analysis: the enormous growth of an international system of needs and their satisfactions, of an international economy. This is the social reality which gives meaning and substance to Freud's mythological account of the growing realm of Eros and the integration of humanity, and it is plainly not fore-seen in Hegel's relatively simple discussion of the nature and basis of international relations. But that is not to say that Hegelian concepts are inadequate to describe it. From a Hegelian point of view, the development of a global eco-nomy, transcending the boundaries of individual states, must pose a very serious problem for the human race; for what kind of state – in Weber's terms, what locus of phys-ical force – can intervene to control it? The institutions that grow out of the attempt to combine society and the market (what Hegel calls 'civil society') imply and require control by a higher, more universal authority (what Hegel calls 'the state'), not least because left to themselves they impoverish and marginalize a section of the population, a mob, which has no interest in the prevailing order except to overthrow it. But, for Hegel, that higher authority can never be a world-state.

The reason why the Hegelian state cannot be a world-state lies deep within the Hegelian system. It lies in Hegel's concept of patriotism, and specifically in what that implies about our sense of our identity. Hegel believes, reasonably enough, that the sense of personal identity, of who, morally speaking, one is, is intimately bound up with the identity of the political, cultural and indeed religious collectivity of which one is a member. Even the poorest Englishman, he says in 1820 in the *Philosophy of Right*, still feels himself to be an Englishman and as such to have rights and freedoms of which he can be proud. The highest possible degree of self-awareness is achieved, Hegel believes, when one becomes aware of oneself as a citizen of one's state, and, conversely, the state itself can only be said to exist when there are individuals who have towards it the 'ethos', the *Gesinnung*, of patriotism. There is only a state in so far as there are people who recognize their society as something they have a duty to die for, if necessary. In saying this, Hegel is not speaking for some sort of inflated or bellicose nationalism – he is only thinking through the implications of the very idea of identity. If identity, the real content of your life, is what you give up only when you die, and if collective and individual identity are inseparably linked, then a collectivity's identity is inseparably linked to what its individual members will die for rather than give up. Patriotism, Hegel remarks, is an everyday virtue: not the humbug of occasional ostentatious emotionalism but

137

the confidence with which one walks the streets in security at night, 'the fundamental feeling of order, common to all'.

Now, it is true that global civil society has developed to a point where there is something like a shared order or expectation of order, for an increasing fraction of the world's population. Increasingly when we say 'we', 'we' means the human race. Increasingly, 'we' are aware of ourselves as a finite natural unity, with finite natural resources. (Hegel would say that our 'we' has the 'moment' of individuality). Increasingly, 'we' are aware of ourselves as a community which has to find ways of reincorporating those whom the economic system, the system for satisfying our mutual needs, threatens to exclude – the global poor. (Hegel would say that our 'we' has the 'moment' of universality). However, what 'we' do not and cannot have is that identity which comes to a community through defining itself over against others of the same kind. (In Hegelian terms, our 'we' lacks the 'moment' of particularity). We cannot constitute ourselves into a world-state, in the full Hegelian sense of the term 'state', because there is, and can by definition be no other world-state in war with which we would feel under a duty to die for our own. (This is one reason for the enduring popularity of science-fiction fantasies of some extraterrestrial threat to the whole world.) World-citizens could not have a sense of patriotism: they could not therefore have a sense of complete identity with the political institutions that represented them, however directly these emerged from global economic life. As we all become less different from one another, we all become less certain of our identity. Patriotism, the readiness to die for an *existing* state, is virtually extinct throughout the world. (Perhaps the Swiss possess it.) The cynics who ask how many are prepared to lay down their lives for Brussels or the UN should be more cynical: how many *more* are prepared to lay down their lives for the land of their birth? Of course, there are many prepared to die, and very many prepared to kill, not, however, for states but for causes and ideas, for religions, for groups (including animals) and for what is called nationalism, that is, the erection or consolidation of states which are at present non-existent or only partially established. That is not patriotism, as Hegel understands it. Loyalty in life and death to a 'feeling of order common to all' has little to do with current events in Iraq, Sudan or Afghanistan. The world political unit, in which our search for collective and personal identity could finally be satisfied, in which we could be freely self-determining citizens, is an idea or cause, too, not a state. It is not, and cannot become, completely real, for in war against whom could its citizens lay down their lives? Globalization is fostering not the growth of a world-state, as the focus of the patriotism of the entire human race, but the growth at an international level of state-like processes, of attitudes, tendencies, and even embryonic institutions, with ambitions to deploy the state-defining power of force in order to achieve the goal of global control, without possessing the universality of an actual state, which would make those ambitions fully effective. We see a worldwide diffusion of the power of force, but as it is not located in authoritative institutions it is brought to bear principally on individuals. The world is indeed unified by violence, but that violence is not fully embodied in global, social institutions and so is not translated into state-like control of our economic behaviour. Instead we have to make do with ethics, and with guilt.

So, for example, we could say that, at the most basic level, the human race possesses the destructive means to wipe itself out, but the power of decision over the use of these weapons with global impact is jealously kept out of the international arena and reserved to national bodies. Given that we have defined the state by its monopoly over force within a particular territory, it is difficult to imagine a planetary force capable of suppressing its rivals without destroying all of us. And it is, frankly, impossible to imagine how such a force could emerge from our present condition of armed disequilibrium. The best we can hope for is that the United States, alone or with others, will lend its support to organizations which have a global reach but can in the end rely for their authority only on economic advantage and moral suasion. The twentieth century saw the welcome growth of a range of international bodies which seek to impose a global order, but they are more convincing the less explicit their appeal to the power of force: the United Nations is less convincing as a global authority than the World Trade Organization, or than its own more specialized humanitarian agencies. The supranational institutions of the European Union go deeper, but on a narrower front, since they are only regional in their ambitions, but even they run into difficulty when defence is an issue or the word 'state' is mentioned. The communications media have a worldwide reach and, as we have seen, bring the power of moralizing aggression, the commands of the super-ego, into every home and soon onto every mobile-phone screen. But those commands lack embodiment in material relations. They are issued by a global authority, such as a world-state might be, but by an authority without any role in our physical or economic life – hence their resemblance to the commands of ethics, as Freud understands them. Only in terrorism, the media's parasitic offshoot, does the moralism of the media make contact with the material power of violence. Terrorism is a consequence of the absence of global institutions to express and impose a consensus about how we are to live together on this planet, but the attempt to deal with it requires from us a degree of cooperation which, we must hope, will eventually bring those institutions into being.

The twentieth century has therefore seen the coincidence of a great increase in the degree of human productive and affective interaction with a corresponding but unfulfilled need for the interaction to be controlled by a state-like deployment of force. In the absence of political institutions on the same scale as the global economy which could be the external agents of the necessary force, force is applied to the individual in the internal form of ethical commands and consequential guilt. But why does the need for an external authority remain unfulfilled so that we have to envisage our personal and collective behaviour being regulated, not by global practices and sanctions, by global legislative, social and executive compulsion, but by a global ethic? In Hegelian terms, why is there no global *Sittlichkeit*, no global ethical *life*, even though there is a global system of needs and satisfactions? I believe the reason lies in a misapprehension, in an as yet rudimentary conception, of the nature of our global political life, conditioned by the self-understanding, or self-misunderstanding, of America, the most powerful repository of physical force in our world.

We have seen that America has given us a great theological fiction about itself, which during the twentieth century came, as a result of American economic and political preeminence, to dominate all thinking about global ethical life: the fiction that it was founded to defend God-given, or at any rate 'unalienable', rights – what the French imitators of the American Revolution declared in 1789 to be the 'natural and imprescriptible' Rights of

Man. Jeremy Bentham, though an admirer of American liberty, thought natural rights a 'simple nonsense', and natural and imprescriptible rights a 'nonsense upon stilts'. One person's 'right', in Bentham's view, existed only as the logical counterpart to someone else's 'duty', and that duty existed only as an obligation imposed by the law, under the threat of force. Nature imposed no laws, and therefore Nature sanctioned no rights: laws issued from the state or, as Bentham put it (in the language of Hobbes), from the sovereign. Yet, despite Bentham's withering critique, human rights flourished and multiplied in the twentieth century as never before. The Universal Declaration of Human Rights, adopted by the United Nations Organization on 10 December 1948, has had, as its drafters intended, numerous progeny in the shape of regional or other more specific declarations or treaties, notably the European Convention on Human Rights of 1950. The Universal Declaration of 1948, inspired by conscientious outrage at the hideous massacres and deportations of the previous two decades, is, within its limits, an admirable document: clear, succinct and practical. Its practical merit, however, is its theoretical weakness – it has no basis. It offers no explanation or derivation for the rights it declares: it just tells us to implement them. The American Declaration of Independence invoked the Creator, the French Declaration of 1789 alluded to the Supreme Being, but the United Nations Organization

143

issued its statement of rights on its own authority or none. The French Thomist philosopher Jacques Maritain, who was on the drafting committee, presumably thought it impolitic or anachronistic to refer to the natural (and so divine) law on which he personally believed rights to be based. Eleanor Roosevelt, however, who chaired the committee, allowed an echo of Jefferson to enter the preamble, which pronounces the rights to be defined 'inalienable'. The echo whispers the truth. The Universal Declaration of 1948 projects onto the world scale the conceptual elision on which the Jeffersonian understanding of the United States Constitution depends: rights are presented as essentially the property of individuals and, like individuals, they precede government: rights are not created by government through its deployment of its monopoly of force. The Declaration is not a treaty between governments, by which they might bind themselves, under sanction, to give certain rights to their citizens. And unlike the European Convention, which set up a commission and a court to give effect to its provisions, it does not set up any institutions – which, given its universal claims, would have to be global. Instead of global institutions, the United Nations in 1948 gave us a global ethic – an ideology of human rights which, nonetheless, like its American model, has at times a thoroughly real application. Just as the Bill of Rights provided ideological cover for the Northern states in their military annexation of the South during the American Civil War, so the doctrine of human rights has provided the justification for (more and less success-ful) interventions by United States power in Africa, the Balkans, Latin America and the Middle East.

This is not to say that these interventions have been unjustifiable on any grounds, and it is certainly not to deny that the Universal Declaration was one of the most hearteningly prophetic signs erected over the desolate landscape of the mid-twentieth century. But it is to say that talk of 'human rights' is a substitute for something else, something concealed by the conceptual elision at its heart – namely, the urgent practical need to promote world governance. The practical need therefore re-emerges in forms that lack, even in American eyes, any systematic justification and are easily denounced as arbitrary or self-serving American adventurism. The enemies of the Declaration recognize this more readily than its friends. The Islamic states that wish to continue to keep slaves, oppress women and suppress religious freedom, and that produce their own declarations of rights that will allow them to do so, like the Chinese and Russian authori-ties who see the appeal to human rights as a pretext for stirring up trouble in their backyards, understand well enough that rights talk is not as harmless as its apparent baselessness might suggest. A right, as Bentham saw, is meaningless unless it emanates from a sovereign with the power and intention to enforce it. Though Americans and others think that in speaking up for human rights they are merely reiterating moral universals, they are in fact either saying nothing or expressing the intention to use their power to impose a global law. The Islamists and the autocrats are correct in assuming that human rights cannot be defended without interference in the internal affairs of what they have learned to call their nation-states. They understand the logic of rights better than those for whom rights are merely, in a half-considered way, indirectly derived from the United States Constitution, the inalienable endowment of the human family. To be committed to universal human rights is, in some sense, to be committed to world governance.

In which sense, then? Even though Hegel is no doubt right and a world-state is an impossibility, condemned to remain always only an idea or a cause, the world-state may still, even as an idea, have a real role in the solution to the problem of world governance. That was clearly seen by Kant, whose thoughts on international order had a deep influence on the founding documents of the European Union and remain of direct contemporary relevance. They also suggest a way in which universal human rights may, after all, be given a real basis.

The concept of a world-state is for Kant what he calls an Idea, and the function of an Idea is to be the point of orientation of all our practical action: it 'regulates', in Kant's term, our actions and our thoughts about actions, in the sense that it tells us what direction we are going in. We lay our course by an Idea, as by a star or by a landmark, not because we want, or are able, to get to the landmark but because we can see it and it will enable us to get to the real goal that we cannot yet see. We lay our course *as if* we could reach the ideal goal, and thereby we reach the next best thing to it. In politics, therefore, international relations must be conducted *as if* they were capable of leading to world-government, even though that goal is, strictly speaking, unattainable and we can be confident of getting ever closer to the ideal state only if we treat it *as if* it were possible to attain it. Kant believed that you could not understand the past unless you had a vision of the future, that the only coherent vision of the human future was that all states should bind themselves into treaty relationships which would prevent war between them, and that in the end only those states which had 'republican' (as we now say, 'democratic') constitutions would be willing to enter on such treaties. Kant certainly did not think that a world of democratic and peaceable states was a probable future for humanity, or even perhaps a goal attainable within a specifiable period of years, but he did think that the only foreseeable alternative is mutual mass destruction – the 'perpetual peace' of the cemetery – and that we need such a goal to define the direction in which we are going, to make sense of our moral lives, that is, of our personal and collective history.

In his treatise *On Perpetual Peace*, Kant seeks to establish what the relation is between the Idea of a world-state and the goal of permanent peace. Ideally, he says, just as individuals put a stop to warring among themselves by jointly submitting themselves to a state authority, so states would cease warring among themselves by jointly submitting to world-government. However, that solution is unrealistically remote, and the practical substitute for world-government – the 'negative surrogate', Kant calls it – has to be a system of international law based on a treaty between states. This Kant calls a 'League of Nations' (*Völkerbund*), since in it the individual states remain intact and are not absorbed into a single world-state. This provides the minimum realization of the goal of permanent peace, since a legal relationship rules out by definition the possibility of recourse to violence, that is, war. However, Kant is quite explicit that while there is every reason to hope and to expect the 'League of Nations' to grow and to include ever more states, such a treaty relation between states may always break down and war may break out again. After all, the twentieth-century League of Nations suffered precisely such a fate. But Kant goes on to argue that certain practical consequences follow, even from the mere existence of the ideal of a world-state. The ideal has an impact even on a world order that is restricted to the negative surrogate for world-government represented by the rule of international law within a 'League of Nations'.

For the legal system that would obtain in the ideal world-state, what Kant calls 'cosmopolitan law', already has to have a certain influence on the legal provisions in the treaty setting up the 'League of Nations'. The cooperation established in the real world must, as a minimum, and at the level of individuals, not of states, allow for a development, an ever-closer approach to the ideal. The interstate, treaty-based law of the 'League of Nations' must at least ensure that individuals are not prevented from engaging in activities that bring the world-state closer. There are, that is, in modern terms, certain human rights whose basis lies not in the law of a particular state but in the idea of a world-state, and those human rights have to be part of the system of international law and have to be provided for in the international treaty that outlaws war between its signatories. Individuals visiting states other than their own have the right to be received as guests, not to be treated inhumanely, expelled or allowed to starve, and they have, most significantly, the right to offer to do business with those who may want to do business with them. Kant sees the spirit of trade as the instrument which brings the peoples of the world together, counters the tendency to war, builds up the international community that makes the treaty of perpetual peace and so advances the human race towards the ultimate ideal of world-government. That ideal is already present among us, and is already affecting our lives, in so far as we give effect, in our own legal systems and through our treaty relations, to universal human rights. The Declaration of 1948, we might say, is a mortgage taken out on the security of our commitment to the Ideal.

The twenty-first century needs global institutions rather than a global ethic. Indeed, a global ethic, properly understood, simply imposes the obligation to establish global institutions. Only the submission of our (largely illusory) nationhood to external, global authorities will relieve us from the guilt and self-destruction imposed on us by the internal authority of the super-ego. It is Kant, rather than Hegel, who shows us how we can emerge from mere ethics into global ethical life. Hegel did not have Kant's understanding of the possibility of a world political system that would be unified but something short of a state in the full sense of the term. The notion that we could at the same time conceive of a goal and know that we cannot attain it – what Kant called having 'ideals' – was anathema to Hegel. Yet this refusal of the future and of what we might call the incompleteness of human life is the weakest point in Hegel's system and the source of all in it that seems unrealistic or objectionable. More than any other of the great philosophers, except perhaps his models Aristotle and Spinoza, Hegel aims to make us feel at home in the world. But the evidence of the century and a half of world history since his death is that though we have a city to build here it is not an abiding one, and that our life has direction rather than a definable purpose. The states that have grown up since the French Revolution cannot be revered, as Hegel requires, 'as something divine on earth', because they are plainly transcended by political or nearly political structures, secular international bodies or supranational religions or other causes, which do not themselves amount to states but which point us, in more or less agreeable ways, towards an ideal of ever-closer cooperation. Maybe the most appealing model for the twenty-first century will be neither the American self-determining nation nor the Chinese imperial bureaucracy but the creatively chaotic yet, in the circumstances, remarkably peaceful example of democratic India. As India opens to the world its potentially enormous economy and consumer base (demographically better structured than China's), so its long traditions of variety, assimilation and a political authority that holds the ring rather than imposing a central will may diffuse outwards to the benefit of everyone.

For all Hegel's insight into the unity of the manifestations of the world spirit, Kant understood better that self-knowledge could not be absolute or perfect but that identity always has to be projected or extrapolated from 'the series of [our completed past] actions' into a future of what we hope or ought to be. If the human race survives the coming century it will be because its members have learnt to see themselves as Kant saw them, as rational beings who are (always) *future* citizens of the world.

Chapter 9

England, Our England: National Identity, Past and Future

Will there be a place for patriotism in the twenty-first century, after the world crisis of the Great Event? If the crisis ushers in a century of major conflict and unbearable ecological stress, local struggles for survival may well generate local assertions of identity. Lacking a relation to the brutal global reality, however, these are unlikely to deserve either the name of 'patriotism' in any Hegelian sense or the attention of serious later thinkers (if there are any). If the crisis is benignly resolved, the question will still arise, and will in some ways be more interesting. But it is a question probably better answered in particular than in general. Home, it has more than once been said, is where one starts from, and I start from England. It is not clear to me that there is such a thing as English patriotism, even now.

In 1941, with enemy bombers flying overhead, George

Orwell wrote down his thoughts on the English identity that he was confident would survive all attempts to destroy it – with the exception, he was prudent enough to add, of prolonged subjugation by a foreign power, which in 1941 was still a distinct possibility. Those thoughts became one of his most famous essays, 'England, Your England', and I looked again at it a while ago, having first read it at a time when it told me, accurately and movingly, what it was to be English, as I then thought I was. What is left of Orwell's analysis of England's enduring character? What is left of England, his England?

> Yes, there *is* something distinctive and recognizable in English civilization [he writes]. It is a culture as individual as that of Spain. It is somehow bound up with solid breakfasts and gloomy Sundays, smoky towns and winding roads, green fields and red pillar boxes.

Anyone of my generation, for whom that sentence is a snapshot, a sudden glimpse out of the corner of the eye, of something they knew in childhood, is likely to be momentarily deceived by it. Yes, we think, that's quite good; there *is* something specially English about the atmosphere it evokes. But look again and you realize that almost all the real physical facts to which it appeals have changed. The red pillar boxes are still just about there,

154

though not, I think, as many as there used to be, and their kindred, evoked by association, the red telephone kiosks and red double-decker buses, are only just holding their own against two determined attempts to destroy them. But as for the rest: solid breakfasts long ago gave way to muesli, so that 'full English breakfast' is now a term of art in catering with about as much relation to England as Kentucky fried chicken has to Kentucky; gloomy Sundays were brightened up by the introduction by Thatcher and Major of the seven-day shopping week; the smoky towns, praise be, became smokeless thanks to the legislation of the 1950s and 1960s, and as the spread of oil and natural gas invalidated the opening sentence of another of Orwell's essays – 'Our civilisation, *pace* Chesterton, is founded on coal', he wrote in 'Down the Mine'. The winding roads may still be there as unimproved B roads, but the motorway network and the dual carriageways have entirely changed our relation to the landscape so that we no longer wend our way through it or in it but travel over, across or past it. You might think that the fields are still green – except that they are more probably yellow with rape – but they are not the small patchwork fields which Orwell had before his mind's eye, divided up by hedgerows, but large tractor-friendly sweeps of standardized crops. In 1941, Orwell thought, no doubt rightly, and no doubt he was in agreement with most English people, that England was different from abroad:

> When you come back to England from any foreign
> country, you have immediately the sensation of
> breathing a different air . . . The beer is bitterer, the
> coins are heavier, the grass is greener, the advertise-
> ments are more blatant . . . However much you hate
> it or laugh at it, you will never be happy away from
> it for any length of time. The suet puddings and the
> red pillar-boxes have entered into your soul.

The green grass we can allow again – though it is, and was
in 1941, greener still in Ireland – but the bitterer beer
has taken second place to the world-conquering lager,
for which the advertisements too are worldwide and not
really culturally distinctive; curry, hamburgers and paella
are more familiar to most English families than suet
puddings; and not only is the coinage only marginally
heavier than the European, if at all: it has been altered so
often in the last 40 years that no one can now experience
that immediate contact with the England of a century or
more ago that came with discovering in your change a
bun-penny or a silver threepenny bit.

What we have witnessed since Orwell wrote his essay
is not, I think, the attrition of a few symbolic and atmos-
pheric details of our lives which happened to be those
he pitched on in order to give a picturesque appeal to
his definition of Englishness. What has happened is that
an entire *Gesinnung*, as Hegel would call it, an ethos of

Englishness has passed away. 'The fundamental feeling of order, common to all.' That, I think, is precisely the sort of self-awareness that Orwell was attributing to the English – as he called them – when he spoke in the same essay of the English sense of English law as 'something above the State', and 1940 was surely the moment in English history when that self-awareness reached its highest possible point. It is surely evident that as the thing which Orwell called England has faded away so too has the willingness to die for it – British soldiers who have died in Iraq have more usually been described by their relatives and friends as doing a job they loved than as laying down their lives for their country – and this parallelism is exactly what Hegel's theory of *Gesinnung* would lead us to expect. What has caused the passing away of that sense of English identity which Orwell described in what someone else at the time called its 'finest hour'? And what is the likely or possible future for the sense of identity of those who once called themselves English?

My answer to the first question is to suggest that what Orwell describes as 'England' is the objective correlative not of a sense of *national* identity but of a sense of *imperial* identity. Of course it doesn't look like that – but hypocrisy about the Empire is, Orwell notes, one of the defining features of Englishness, and, indeed, in at least one important respect he shares it himself, as we shall see in a moment. With great percipience he compares England to 'a family, a rather stuffy Victorian family, with not many black sheep in it but with all its cupboards bursting with skeletons. It has rich relations who have to be kowtowed to and poor relations who are horribly sat upon, and there is a deep conspiracy of silence about the source of the family income'. What that conspiracy of silence is concealing is that what are thought of as permanent and character-istic features of English life are in reality mainly respects in which an antiquated and vestigially feudal society is insulated from processes of modernization which have already overtaken other European states, not to mention America.

In 1940, and, thanks to victory, even after 1945, Britain was still a pre-revolutionary society, the last in Europe. The medieval institutions had been adapted but were largely intact. What made possible this time warp, this preservation of a Lost World, was the Empire. That was the protective insulation, economic, political, cultural and demographic, which accounted for that feeling of difference when Orwell stepped off his ferry from Europe and breathed the English air. Just as the French Empire, a nineteenth-century creation, preserved the great fic-tion of the Revolutionary and Napoleonic era – that France was and could remain an integrated, centralized, autarkic state – so the British Empire preserved England's haphazard and pre-rational constitution. Economically, the Empire provided the protected markets that founded many a family fortune; politically the white and non-white inhabitants of the Empire provided a body of lesser breeds by contrast with which even the poorest Englishman, as Hegel noted, could identify himself as *civis Romanus* and know he had rights and freedoms; culturally, the Empire created an entire world in which the English language and the English church, the antiquated English currency, English mensuration and English cuisine all could establish themselves without competition and without serious question as the norm; and demographically, the Empire provided a virtually unrestricted career structure for the ambitious and a generously administered escape route for the discontented and the criminal. Orwell shares in the conspiracy of silence, in so far as he thinks he is defining what it is to be English when he is actually defining what it is to be a metropolitan of the British Empire. That this is so is shown by his uncertainty – an uncertainty shared by most later writers on the subject – as to who the English actually are, whom the term refers to. In the first instance one would have thought the English were native inhabitants of the British Isles who were not Scottish or Irish or Welsh. It is a serious weakness of Orwell's essay that he does not consider whether there might be specifically Scottish, Welsh or, especially, Irish perspectives on the culture he is describing and on the particular emblems he uses to characterize it. It is not merely a trivial oversight that he does not notice that the grass is greener in Ireland than it is in England. He probably thinks, at a half-conscious level, that Ireland is part of England and that the real point is that 'our' grass is greener than the European. Indeed, he virtually says as much when he refers to 'the fact that *we* [my emphasis] call *our islands* [my emphasis] by no less than six different names, England, Britain, Great Britain, the British Isles, the United Kingdom and, in very exalted moments Albion'. Even in 1940, no citizen of the Irish Free State would have regarded the island of Ireland as referred to by any of these terms except possibly 'the British Isles'. The 'we' here, who lay claim to 'our islands', evidently have a distinctly Imperial attitude to Great Britain's western neighbour. Now Orwell's 'hesitation' shows, I think, that the culture he is defining does not have the physical and geographical specificity that he is claiming for it. It is not the culture of a nation. It is part of the self-image of one of world history's great ruling classes. The English long ago gave up any local identity they might have had in order to devote themselves to that Imperial venture, and if they are now seeking an historically based identity they will have to look back not – as many still do – to 1940 and the war with Germany but to a period before England gave up trying to be a nation and set out to turn itself into an Empire instead.

Having such an intangible and characterless past, England may have a certain advantage – the advantage of an intellectual clarity unclouded by inherited prejudice – when it comes to asking what its identity, or anybody's identity, is likely to be in the future. One thing is certain. Identity will not, for any other than touristic and sporting purposes, have much to do with being a nation. If we ask what are the forces that have rendered obsolete Orwell's emblems of Englishness, they are all forces to which national boundaries are increasingly irrelevant – trade, travel and competition. It was the imperatives of international competition that forced on Britain the renewal of the transport infrastructure – the building of the motorways and the pruning of the railways, the obliteration of Orwell's winding roads and the closing of Adlestrop. The forces of international competition that substituted imported gas and oil for home-mined coal have also rationalized away those little fields; just as the search for profitability of increasingly international business groups led the supermarkets to press for Sunday opening. The advent of mass holiday travel in the 1960s and 1970s changed the eating habits of the British at the same time as the increasing volume and ease of trade made foreign beers and wines available to change their taste in drink. In the age of email, it requires no great prescience to doubt whether the red pillar boxes will see out another century.

Orwell's England came and went with Britain's Empire. The last 130 years or so have seen the rise of numerous colonial empires as attempts to give political shape to the nascent global market; and in the Seventy-Five Years' War, from 1914 to 1989, those empires were destroyed by the same global market. But the processes which came to a climax and a catastrophe from 1870 onwards had their origins in much earlier phases of European history. In the case of England, the process of empire-building started no later than the sixteenth century, when a number of the developments which culminated in the late nineteenth century took their origin: the new definition of the nation through the breaking of religious ties with Rome; the triumph of the central bureaucracy, at first peaceably under Henry VII, then with Maoist savagery through the cultural revolutions of Henry VIII and Edward VI; the establishment of a colonial relation with Ireland and, at first less successfully, with Scotland, as well, of course, as overseas; and consequently the first beginnings of that uncertainty about the national identity which continues down to our own day as the question 'are we English? Or British?'

It follows that if we want to know what our nation and our culture might be in the aftermath of Empire we should look back to the period before the sixteenth-century empire-building began. And there in the later Middle Ages we will find the nearest thing to a historical precedent for the Europe that began to reveal itself to us when communism collapsed before the onrushing tide of globalization: a Europe made up of an extraordinary variety of political units, from kingdoms and duchies to cities and bishoprics, corresponding to neither cultural nor linguistic divisions and coexisting with larger-scale economic and juridical entities, such as the Hanseatic League or the Holy Roman Empire. 'Nation' in the fifteenth century was a term which probably applied to no single political entity in Europe. Far from referring to some basic unit of human association, which provided an aboriginal definition of those who belonged to it, *natio* was a word naturally used in the context of universities or of the church, to refer to a group, loosely united by geographical or linguistic connections, who made up a part of some *larger* whole – the 'nations' were, for example, the constituent fractions of the delegates to the Council of Constance. That sense that the nations are subsidiaries of, and derivative from, some larger underlying unity is, I have suggested in this book, a feature of the postmodern and post-imperial world, yet it was also a feature of European life 600 years ago when the underlying unity was not Microsoft or global banking but Christendom. That world of mercenaries and wandering scholars, when French was still written in England and Latin was spoken everywhere, can provide us with an example of how it is possible to live, and think of yourself, both as originating in a particular place or culture and as a member of a universal order, ecclesiastical or even, in the case of the Empire, secular.

In the moment of Henry's breach with Rome the fracturing of Christendom began. Over the centuries

Christendom gave way to a Europe, and eventually a world, made up of what America has taught us to call nations, supposedly autonomous and autochthonous, the objects of an idolatrous worship. But the false gods have died, the gods of the nations. Does this mean that we must now hope for the mending of what was broken, the reconstruction, at least in Europe, of the Christendom that was shattered in the sixteenth century? The question became live when the preamble to a European Constitution was hotly discussed, and it has not disappeared with the demise of that ill-fated document.

I think the answer must be both no and yes. No, because the past can never be recovered and because no mere fraction of the physical planet, not even a fraction as large as the geographical unit that was once Christendom, can be the medium through which we as consumer-producers in a global economy can expect to find ourselves. Such identity as we now have is global, and the old Christendom had a less than global reach. Yes, because the spirit of the Christendom that fell apart in the sixteenth century is a universal spirit, and a new Christendom would be capable of expressing a universal identity and so of expressing what we now truly are. That is not, of course, to say that the new Christendom must somehow be synonymous or coterminous with the European Union. That is precluded by the nature both of Europe and of Christendom.

The Europe that very largely coincided with the old

Christendom had definite geographical and cultural boundaries. It stopped clearly at the Atlantic and the Hellespont, somewhat less clearly somewhere east of Kiev, and it certainly did not include the Islamic world, except provisionally as the invading or occupying Turk or Moor. The political structure of the new Europe already all but fills out the boundaries of the old, and already we know that in concept and in principle it transcends them. It is thinkable that one day Russia could be an applicant for membership of the Union, and to think that thought is to recognize that at a stroke Europe could acquire a Pacific coastline. (Indeed, in a sense it already has one, since Russia is a member of the Council of Europe.) More immediate, and more fundamental, is the prospect raised by the application of Europe's long-standing adversary Turkey, the accession of which would seem finally to destroy the link between Europe and old Christendom. But it would be an enlargement of Europe entirely in accordance with the spirit of variety and collegiality which is Europe's answer to the American ideology of the melting pot. And if Turkey, why not, one day, Israel (already a contributor to the Eurovision Song Contest)? The process of economic and political pacification and coordination that is Europe's ever-closer union has no clear or necessary territorial or cultural bounds. It will stop only when the supply of applicants dries up. It can be envisaged as a multifaith, multicultural, multispeed and multilevel union of former nations, bound together by their commitment to three things, all equally important: the free market, democracy (that is, political liberty and the right to vote) and the rule of supranational institutions (the commitment which distinguishes Europe from the USA).

And Christendom? How might we begin to envisage a new Christendom of which England might be a member as it once was of the old? For Christians themselves that should not be a difficult question to answer. The world-wide church is one of humanity's truly global institutions. The church can speak, whether at the level of local communities, or of nations or of the EU itself, for those who are not part of the cycle of production and consumption – for those who cannot work, whether through disability or unemployment or those whose work, in bearing and bringing up children, for example, is not rewarded with the power to consume – and for those aspects of creation (human, animal, vegetable or mineral) that are not agents in the process of production and consumption though they may be profoundly affected by it or even be its material: the life of human feeling, for example, that is refined or degraded by the media; the animals and plants that we feed on or exploit; the biosphere and the landscape that we alter, functionalize or pollute. For those who are detached from Christianity, however, but who can recognize themselves as future world-citizens, the key to our future identity is perhaps to be found in language.

Christendom was a linguistic as well as a religious and geographical community. No doubt the common language of the future European union, especially as it grows, will, for all practical purposes, be the language of the USA. But this common language will not be as it is in the USA the language that binds a nation together in monoglottal insularity. It will be, as Latin once was in the old Christendom, the shared medium of those who come from and return to their own home tongues at either end of the working day. It will be another supranational institution mediating between the global market and the territories and traditions of former nations and so in its own way a means of preserving variety and neighbourliness. In the preface to his translation of *Beowulf*, Seamus Heaney writes inspiringly about the apparent paradox that he, an Irish poet and nationalist, should want to translate a literary monument of Ireland's Anglo-Saxon oppressors, and about his (literally, or metaphorically literally) intoxicating discovery of the delights of polyglossy – of the linguistic and cultural landscape which was there before national boundaries were drawn, before languages and states were thought to be necessarily coextensive, and which, I would add, may yet come again as the boundaries, like East Germany's wall and fence, fade back into the grass. Having long conceived of English and Irish as 'adversarial tongues', he learned as a student in lectures on the history of the English language that the word 'whiskey' is the same word as the Gaelic word *uisce*, meaning water, and that the River Usk (also originally Uisce) in Britain is therefore in a sense the River Whiskey:

> The Irish/English duality, the Celtic/Saxon anti-thesis were momentarily collapsed and in the resulting etymological eddy a gleam of recognition flashed through the synapses and I glimpsed an elsewhere of potential that seemed at the same time to be a somewhere being remembered [. . .]. What I was experiencing was the feeling that Osip Mandelstam once defined as a 'nostalgia for world culture'.

The new Europe will provide an image of that 'world culture', both as a past 'somewhere remembered' and as a future 'elsewhere of potential': where one day perhaps all the world can be a place of variety and tolerant hospitality in which the Hungarians will keep what I believe they call their 'Farmers' as the Germans will keep their 'Handys' while the French continue to holiday on 'le camping' and the English continue to live in their 'cul-de-sacs' and to eat 'al fresco'. It will be a house with many mansions, most of which will not be recognizable to those who dwelt in the nations of the past, but it will seem like home to those whose synapses can recall the still older Christendom.

Index

Index